MARRIAGE, MURDER, & BETRAYAL

IN NINETEENTH-CENTURY

CALIFORNIA

Marriage, Murder, & Betrayal

in Nineteenth-Century

California

JO M. HARAF

AMERICA
THROUGH TIME®
ADDING COLOR TO AMERICAN HISTORY

*To my husband William for his
unwavering support in all things*

America Through Time is an imprint of Fonthill Media LLC
www.through-time.com
office@through-time.com

Published by Arcadia Publishing by arrangement with Fonthill Media LLC
For all general information, please contact Arcadia Publishing:
Telephone: 843-853-2070
Fax: 843-853-0044
E-mail: sales@arcadiapublishing.com
For customer service and orders:
Toll-Free 1-888-313-2665

www.arcadiapublishing.com

First published 2021

Copyright © Jo M. Haraf 2021

ISBN 978-1-63499-347-0

Typeset in 10pt on 13pt Sabon
Printed and bound in England

Contents

Acknowledgments

Internet newspaper and genealogy sites make excellent jumping-off points for in-depth research. Newspapers.com, the California Digital Newspaper Collection (www.cdnc.ucr.edu), Ancestry.com, and FamilySearch.org provided great context and links for further exploration.

Libraries, historical societies, and museums graciously opened their collections for review. The Bancroft Library, University of California, Berkeley, allowed me ungloved access to ledgers and letters that were over a century old. I am indebted to the Anne T. Kent California Room in the Marin County Library for many documents, especially the *San Francisco Bulletin*'s daily columns on the fourth Black will trial. The Society of California Pioneers, Nicasio Historical Society, Jack Mason Museum of West Marin History, Peter Benitz family, and the California State Archives loaned many illustrations.

Many people supported this endeavor from concept to completion. Jean Harkee Mansen, my editor and friend, too many times dropped everything to critique my text and answer numerous detailed questions. Any errors remaining in the book are due to my ignoring her expert advice. Linda Ruggeri translated Spanish wills, hunting certificates, and other details of nineteenth-century life. My early readers (Fred Melton, Heather Powell, Michal Strutin, and Dewey Livingston) each brought a unique perspective to *Marriage, Murder, and Betrayal in Nineteenth-Century California*. Their advice improved my prose, corrected my errors, and convinced me that the Black family still had a story to tell.

My greatest appreciation goes to the Marin History Museum and Heather Powell, collections manager. Heather's enthusiasm, research, and photography inspired and illustrated this book.

Introduction

The Marin History Museum's storage rooms might resemble your grandparents' attic or hayloft. Elk antlers dangle from a post. Nipper, a relic from the 1915 Panama-Pacific International Exposition, still listens for "his master's voice." Wagon wheels, 3 feet across, hang from the ceiling like oak cobwebs. Wood-framed backpacks, last worn in pre-World War II arctic expeditions, recline on steel shelves mere feet from the ephemera of a nineteenth-century boys' military academy.

When the museum prepares for its semi-annual acquisition review, new treasures and a few questionable artifacts blanket every flat surface. As I wandered through the pre-review maze, the portrait of a young woman caught my eye. Dark hair, intricately braided and twisted into ringlets, crowned her left-facing oval profile. She wore a black taffeta dress with a small white collar and a large black bow. I sensed a woman of beauty as well as privilege and strength.

"Who is she?" I asked.

"That's Augustina," the collections manager responded. "She ate her father's will."

Those five words—"she ate her father's will"—sent me on a three-year journey to learn all I could about Maria Augustina Black, her family, and her times.

Although I made every effort to ascertain the true facts of the Black family's time in California, this book is a work of literary nonfiction—facts told as a story, not an exacting history. In my research and writing, I relied on nineteenth-century publications along with handwritten journals. Quoted dialogue comes from reliable sources such as letters, account books, biographies, and newspaper reports, including the *San Francisco Evening Bulletin*'s many columns on the fourth Black will trial. I used secondary sources and local lore where original documents were scarce. In my efforts to provide a sense of place, I offer descriptions that are likely true, but unverifiable. For example, I suggest the family endured foggy summer mornings. After living in Marin County for twenty-five years, I guarantee you that "Fogust," the month between July and September, lives up to its damp and gray reputation.

Research can be a mind-numbing, fruitless exercise. I spent hours in the cloistered reading room of the University of California Berkeley's Bancroft Library, fighting sleep while translating the fading nineteenth-century penmanship in ancient account books

Above: Marin History Museum.
(*Heather Powell*)

Left: Maria Augustina Black.
(*Marin History Museum*)

and personal records, occasionally energized by a rare find—how I wanted to stand on my chair, holler, and wave a 160-year-old shopping list gaily in the air. Alas, any one of those actions would have had me shushed and expelled.

In these pages, I spare you the minutiae of my research, no matter how much I want to share every single dead-end and fireworks-worthy success. Instead, in nine short tales, we will explore how the Black family matured alongside California, with both the family and the state becoming wealthy and notorious along the way.

1

James Black Arrives

For there to be a Black family in Marin County, there must first be a father, and as that father was born in Scotland, he must make his way to California—decades before California was an American state.

James Black, Jr., was born on New Year's Day, 1810, in Hamilton, Scotland, a village south of the industrial and cultural centers of Glasgow and Edinburgh. Black's parents moved James and his two sisters, Margaret and Jane, to Liverpool, where Black, Sr., took work as a master of the docks. In 1831, James Black followed his father to sea and shipped out on a Hudson Bay Company vessel bound for the Pacific Northwest's seemingly inexhaustible supply of sea otter pelts.

From Callao, Peru, he wrote home that he had signed on aboard the two-masted Mexican brigantine *Catalina*, bound for California. Responding to letters from home, he wrote of his joy "to hear of sister Margaret's union with Mr. Jones. Give them my best respects, wishing them much joy with health and happiness in store." He anticipated, "the pleasure of meeting with you all in about sixteen months, perhaps a little more. I am sorry that we have been parted so long."

Black had no cause to celebrate his twenty-second birthday on January 1, 1832. Sailing north up the California coast on board the *Catalina,* he had seen the corpses of men who had died from ship's fever (likely typhus) tossed overboard, their leather trunks containing the sum of their lives following their owners to the deep. Perhaps there had been enough Protestant left in him that he had muttered a word or two of prayer for their souls.

New Year's Day was Black's turn to sweat and shiver in his hammock below decks. He had vomited his last meal the day before but had no thought of eating, not that anyone would come close enough to offer him food or comfort. Lying in clothes soiled by stool more blood than substance, Black knew that his death meant he would join his shipmates on the ocean floor. Monterey was near, and he realised that he must stay alive until the *Catalina* made port.

The next day, the captain ordered Black and his trunk to be dumped on Monterey's beach, promising to come back if the sailor survived. The ship never returned for its stranded sailor.

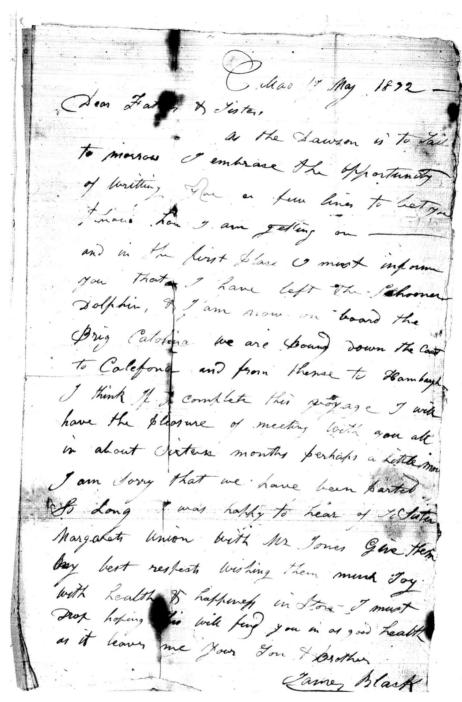

James Black's letter home from Callao, Peru, of May 17, 1832. (*Burdell-Black family papers, BANC MSS C-B 952 Part II, The Bancroft Library, University of California, Berkeley*)

James Black. (*Charmaine Burdell Collection, Jack Mason Museum*)

Monterey, the capital of Mexico's colony in Alta (Upper) California, is perched delicately on the barb of its 24-mile fishhook-shaped bay. In *Two Years Before the Mast* (1840), Richard Henry Dana, Jr., the Harvard student turned sailor, proclaimed Monterey "the prettiest town on the coast." The Pacific Ocean deposited endless waves upon the shore, pushing sandpipers inland past beached and bleached whale bones, then pulling the birds back to fight over the whales' remains. The relentless ocean wind tortured the shoreline's live oaks into flattened silhouettes while groves of pine trees festooned with moss layered the inland hills with green corduroy. Flocks of gulls and geese, drifting through air scented with pine and brine, cast broad shadows on the sand.

Self-important with the only licensed customs house on the west coast as well as a Mexican military *presidio*, Monterey served as the region's commercial and governmental center. Mud streets fronted a dozen or so single-story, whitewashed adobe homes topped by red-tiled roofs. The homes appeared randomly dropped, as if tossed by a child playing with seashells. Thin winter sun glanced off glass windows in the homes of the wealthy while the less well-to-do covered the gaps in their walls with iron grates, wooden lattice, or nothing at all.

In 1826, six years before Black was abandoned on shore, Monterey's population totaled 114 civilians plus the Mexican garrison. One of those civilians was John Rogers Cooper, who had arrived in Monterey three years earlier as captain of the schooner *Rover*. After his arrival, the captain boarded with Ignacio Vallejo, his eventual

The city of Monterey, 1842. (*Courtesy of the California History Room, California State Library, Sacramento, California*)

father-in-law. Cooper stood a slight 5 feet, 5 inches tall with a useless, twisted left hand. His sandy hair and blue eyes contrasted with the appearance of his Mexican wife, Maria Jerónima de la Encarnación Vallejo. Encarnación brought to her marriage virginity, religion, and a brother destined to be a military commandant and governor of Mexican California. Considered a "dependable, law-abiding, substantial" man with a religious wife, Cooper took the ailing Black into his home.

While caring for two children under five years old, two sisters, a ten-year-old niece, a brother-in-law, and his fiancée, Cooper's wife nursed Black to health, washing and feeding him while she prayed. Encarnación spoke no English and Black's Spanish, if he had any, must have been incomprehensible through his Scottish burr. Bowls of Encarnación's posole soup restored Black's body. Resting on wind-dried sheets, his spirit healed while Encarnación, her bowed head often covered in a lace cap, read aloud from her Spanish Bible.

Cooper once wrote a friend, "The people I am acquainted with remain the same as usual, but my wife she grows better every day, that is my opinion," a judgment Black would have affirmed with a hearty "aye."

In time, Black grew stronger. Soups and teas gave way to beefsteaks and whisky. Eventually, Cooper introduced Black to another Scotsman, Edward McIntosh, who had sailed with Cooper on the *Rover*. In short order, the highlander McIntosh and the

Juan Bautista Rogers Cooper. (*BANC PIC 2007.47--CASE, The Bancroft Library, University of California, Berkeley*)

Maria Geronima de la Encarnación Vallejo Cooper. (*The Society of California Pioneers*)

lowlander Black established a close kinship. McIntosh appeared in Cooper's 1829–1831 retail account books as purchasing shirts, jackets, "chockolate," cigars, and various other sundries.

One can imagine the two mates seated on substantial stools of whale vertebrae—furniture being a scarce luxury—comparing histories and pondering their futures over a wee dram of whisky. Black took to calling McIntosh, twenty-six years his senior, "Old Mac." Perhaps Old Mac developed a fatherly attitude toward Black, or possibly he longed for a companion whose accent neared his own. In any case, Old Mac settled the question of their immediate future when he offered Black a job.

2

McIntosh's Journey

Over 100 years before either James Black or Old Mac arrived in California, the British had sown the seeds for the Scottish diaspora. After defeating the Scots in the Battle of Culloden on April 16, 1746, the victorious British undertook to systematically dismantle Scottish culture.

Speaking Gaelic was outlawed. Bagpipes fell silent. Donning a kilt, or any tartan cloth, earned six months in prison. A second offense earned seven years of hard labor. With marriages forbidden among estate tenants, the unwanted Scottish population shrank. British sheep grazed on former Scottish farms. Burned out of their homes, farmers fled to the barren coast to carve out a subsistence living on rocky slivers of land, using seaweed for fertilizer.

We do not know why Old Mac left the land of his birth, but we know the route he followed. The Scots are a seafaring people. From the North Sea to the North Atlantic, the ocean washes more than 6,000 miles of the Scottish coast. Generations spent working the sea gave the Scots a low-cost, hard-work path to escape English persecution by manning the trading company ships sailing the globe in search of profits. The 1820s alone saw an estimated 3,100 Scots settling in the twenty-four United States. Among them was forty-year-old Edward McIntosh, who, in 1823, sailed with Captain John Rogers Cooper on the *Rover* around South America's Cape Horn to Monterey, the main trading port of the former Spanish colony, now Mexican Alta California.[1]

McIntosh quickly adopted the local Mexican customs and practices. On Christmas Eve, 1828, he converted to Catholicism at Mission San Carlos Borromeo del Río Carmelo, now Carmel Mission, his first step toward becoming a naturalized Mexican citizen. As was the expectation, he adopted a Spanish middle name: Edward Manuel McIntosh. As the years went on, "Edward" took second place leaving Manuel Edward McIntosh to go forward.

Edward Manuel McIntosh's baptism. (*Archives of the Diocese of Monterey*)

3
Making a Living in California

Nineteenth-century Chinese royalty developed a lust for sensuous sea otter robes and fur belts trimmed with pearls. Always eager to turn a profit, British, American, and Russian traders crammed their ships' holds with hundreds of skins and sailed to China. In Canton (Gaungzhou), sea otter fur sold for more than six times the cost of beaver or land otter skins. In 1832, the price for a single "soft gold" hide reached $75 (Spanish dollars). In the early 1800s, Spanish and American dollars traded at par, meaning that solitary precious pelt sold for $1,944 in 2019 dollars.

In April 1827, four months before his marriage to Encarnación, John Rogers Cooper was baptized at San Carlos Church in Monterey becoming Juan Bautista Rogers Cooper, possibly inspired by the nearby Mission San Juan Bautista. Catholicism was a requirement to become a naturalized Mexican citizen and, most likely, a non-negotiable requirement to become Encarnación's husband. Naturalized three years later, Cooper was at the front of the line when the Mexican government issued sea otter hunting licenses to its citizens and naturalized foreigners. Once, he bagged 700 skins in a single season. By 1833, overhunting meant he took only thirty-two otters. Recognizing the near extinction of sea otters, he predicted, "I do not think we shall get six hundred in all of the coast."

McIntosh also became a Mexican citizen in 1833 and received a four-month license to hunt sea otters from San Luis Obispo Mission to the Port of Bodega starting on November 20, 1834. The license included the usual provision against harvesting juvenile otters and required the crew to consist of two-thirds Mexican citizens. McIntosh invited James Black and Job Francis Dye, a naturalized Mexican, to join him in the now marginally profitable business of selling otter pelts to the British Hudson Bay Company. In an article written years later, Dye recalled, with some irritation, the unfavorable financial agreement he had made with McIntosh. "I killed eighteen otter and McIntosh one, and the profits were equally divided between us." There was no word on Black's hunting prowess.

Sea otters, floating on their backs, their short arms linked, covered the water in what the trappers called rafts. After over-hunting decimated the rafts, leaving only scattered pairs and small family groups, McIntosh, Black, and Dye needed another line of work.

Left: Sea otter. *(@istockphoto/Neal Aronson)*

Below: Sea otter skins. *(University of Washington Libraries, Special Collections, SOC0759)*

McIntosh's sea otter hunting permit. (*Burdell-Black family papers, BANC MSS C-B 952 Part II, The Bancroft Library, University of California, Berkeley*)

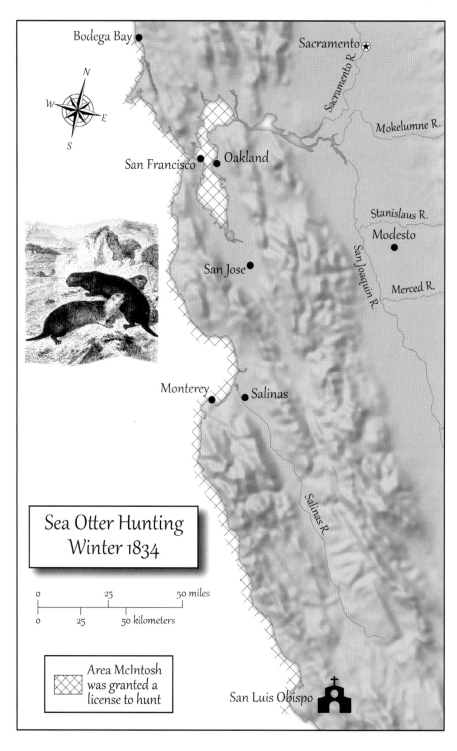

Bodega Bay

Sacramento

Sacramento R.

Mokelumne R.

N
W   E
S

San Francisco • Oakland

Stanislaus R.
Modesto

San Joaquin R.

San Jose

Merced R.

Monterey • Salinas

Salinas R.

Sea Otter Hunting
Winter 1834

```
0          25          50 miles
0      25      50 kilometers
```

Area McIntosh
was granted a
license to hunt

San Luis Obispo

(*Mary Rostad*)

They joined the new business of buying cowhides from the region's burgeoning herd of ranchers and selling them to merchant companies to be made into shoes, belts, and other accessories. In *Two Years Before the Mast* (1840), Richard Henry Dana, Jr., recalled how Monterey, in the mid-1830s, had "no credit system, no banks, and no way of investing money but in cattle. Besides silver, they have no circulating medium but hides, which the sailors call California bank-notes." Valued at $2 each ($50 in 2019), the unwieldy cowhides were used to make purchases from traveling merchant ships, exchanged with local tradesmen, and reportedly used to pay Mexican taxes.[2]

While McIntosh and Black were harvesting the last of the sea otters, the Russian-American Company, founded by the Russian emperor in 1799, turned from hunting otter fur to annexing California land. In 1812, the Russians established Fort Ross (or Russ) 90 miles north of San Francisco at the mouth of the Slavianka (now Russian) River. *The Sonoma Democrat*, quoting a July 4, 1876, speech celebrating California's history, described the Russians as "the pioneer 'squatters' of California." Firmly established on what was then Spanish land, Fort Ross's wooden stockade enclosed houses (some with glass windows and carpets), a chapel, and a water well for emergencies. Farms, a shipyard, brickworks, and a tannery made the settlement near self-supporting. From their fortified base, the Russians made hunting forays southward into San Francisco Bay.

Upon Fort Ross's inception, the then Spanish commanders of Alta California initiated a diplomatic dance to evict the Russians. Unfortunately, the Russians were not willing waltz partners. First, the Spanish reminded the Russians that they had never been given permission to settle in California. In response, Commander Ivan Kuskov stomped his wooden leg and forwarded the dispatch to his superiors in Russia, burying the Spanish plea in the Russian

Fort Ross. (*Courtesy of the California History Room, California State Library, Sacramento, California*)

bureaucracy. Next, given a document showing that the fort violated the Spanish-Russian treaty, Kuskov replied that he could not read Spanish. Perhaps a Russian translation was possible? In 1815, the Spanish again insisted Kuskov abandon the fort. In what amounted to a diplomatic nose-thumbing, Kuskov expanded the Russian's landholdings around Fort Ross.

In 1821, nearly a decade after the Russian fort first appeared, Mexico declared independence from Spain. The governor of the new Mexican Republic demanded the fort be abandoned within six months. Realizing his military and political weaknesses, and hoping to control what he could not contain, the governor granted the Russians permission to hunt—but no farther south than San Francisco Bay. One year later, the Russians hunted San Pedro Bay, 350 miles south of San Francisco. Uninvited and unwelcome, the Russians were guests who would not leave.

Mexico may have ceded the coast to Russia, but the land battle was still to be fought. In the meteoric rise soldiers experience in times of war and conquest, Mexico's governor, Jose Figueroa, promoted Cooper's brother-in-law, Lieutenant Mariano Guadalupe Vallejo, to general and military commander and director of colonization of the Northern Frontier. On June 24, 1835, Vallejo received a secret memo from Figueroa in which the governor warned of the danger from "our neighbors to the north."[3] Figueroa stressed the importance of protecting Bodega Bay and Mendocino from the Russians, as both locations were "of so much interest for the preservation of [Mexican] national integrity."

Figueroa instructed Vallejo to build a wall of homesteading colonizers between the Russians and San Francisco. Figueroa reasoned that if the Russians crossed Mexican-occupied land on their way to San Francisco, their actions would constitute an invasion, after which he could respond with his *presidio*-based garrison of soldiers. Vallejo's success, the governor asserted, would assure the twenty-eight-year-old general "the award to which all men aspire: Posthumous Fame." As Vallejo had already demonstrated an appreciation for corporal rewards, it is reasonable to expect that other, more tangible, inducements were made.

With the Russians knock, knock, knockin' on San Francisco's Bay, Vallejo deployed non-native Mexicans as the vanguard of his homestead barrier. Foreigners and naturalized Mexicans would take the risks, sparing the native Mexicans from harm. Risks are normally partnered with rewards, and in this instance, Vallejo enticed his volunteers with land. At the recommendation of his brother-in-law, Vallejo recruited Black, McIntosh, and Irishman James Dawson to move into the Bodega region between Fort Ross and San Francisco. For their 1835 journey north, the trio purchased gear from Cooper's Monterey store, including items they could not shoot or fashion for themselves: a boat, a knife, a pair of boots, several tubs of grog, 4 pounds of tobacco, and a single box of meal. It is pleasant to imagine the men, after a hard day taming the land, relaxing by a fire with a mug of grog, surrounded by a halo of tobacco smoke.

Colonizers in place, Vallejo sought the land he promised to bestow on the three men and the others who followed them. Conveniently, on November 20, 1833, the Mexican Congress "absorbed" the fertile and well-tended mission lands from the founding religious orders. Governors and military commanders, often the same person, had the power to grant appropriated mission land to those who performed a service for the government. The most generous grants spanned eleven Spanish leagues, equaling nearly 50,000 acres at 4,428.34 acres per league.

The Days of the Dons, the landed gentry, was close at hand.

General Mariano Guadalupe Vallejo. (*Courtesy of the California History Room, California State Library, Sacramento, California*)

4

Making a Home in Marin

In 1841, after ignoring three decades of being told to "GO HOME," the Russians finally abandoned Fort Ross, illegally selling what was not theirs to John Sutter, whose mill would launch the gold rush seven years later. With the Russians gone, General Vallejo awarded Black, McIntosh, and Dawson their expected land grants—pending approval by the governor—and such land they were granted. J. P. Munro-Fraser, in his *History of Marin County California* (1880), described Marin in the early 1840s:

> The country, in whatever valley soever we walked, was an interminable grain field; mile upon mile, acre after acre, wild oats grew in marvelous profusion, in many places to prodigious height … high over head of the wayfarer on foot and shoulder high with the equestrian; wild flowers of every prismatic shade charmed the eye … The air filled with the hum of bees, the chirrup of birds, and an overpowering fragrance from the various plants weighted the air.

Wild cattle (escapees from the Mission San Raphael) mingled with thousands of elk and antelope. Coyotes chased rabbits, sending up flights of quail. Munro-Fraser considered Marin the "noblest work of God."

Black's grant covered the 10,786-acre Rancho Cañada de Jonive, approximately 10 miles northwest of Bodega Bay, where he built an adobe home on the western base of Jonive Hill.[4] On March 8, 1840, he traveled 45 miles south to Mission San Raphael Arcángel in San Rafael for his Catholic baptism. Three years later, Santiago Black became a naturalized Mexican citizen.

Old Mac and Dawson's 8,849-acre Rancho Estero Americano (also called Cañada de Mais), named for its estuary where the river meets saltwater, shared a northeast boundary corner with Black's land. In time, Old Mac and Dawson built a redwood house they intended to share and recorded their homestead in a hand-drawn map (also known as a *diseño*). *Diseños* documented land claims using nature—such as rivers, creeks, mountains, rock outcroppings, and trees—to define boundaries between properties. Dirt roads, houses, neighbors, and local place names often contributed to the penciled sketch.

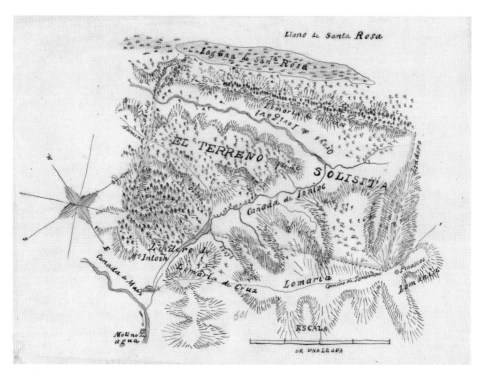

Black's land: Cañada de Jonive. Note "McIntosh" and drawn homestead are in the lower left corner. (*California State Archives, Diseños Collection, Diseño 11601*)

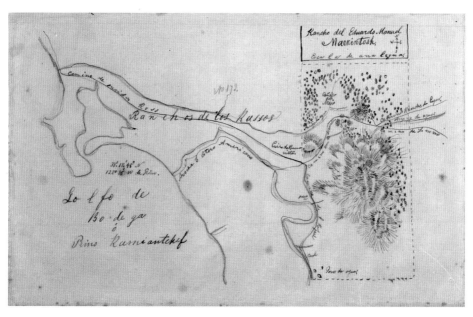

"Diseño Estero Americano/Rancho del Edwards Manuel Mackintosh [*sic*.]." Note: Ranchos de los Russos. (*California State Archives, Disñeos Collection, Diseño 11322*)

In 1839, McIntosh, *diseño* in hand, traveled south to request a joint title to his and Dawson's common land. In Monterey, he learned Mexico did not issue shared land grants. When he returned to the rancho with a land grant, in his name only, an infuriated Dawson "flogged" his former friend, according to H. H. Bancroft. In a heroic feat of carpentry, Dawson reportedly sawed the newly constructed house in half, relocating his portion to the neighboring Rancho Cañada de Pogolimi, which is near today's Bloomfield, California.[5]

In his second will dated December 30, 1844, Old Mac affirmed his intention to "bequeath to Santiago Black all the property specified in [his first] will, together with all the property which I may have accumulated since the date of said [will]." Old Mac's wills represent two of the rare instances where Black is referred to in writing as "Santiago."

For ready money, Black left Jonive to log trees at Cooper's Rancho San Quentin on San Francisco Bay.[6] While working, he met a *señorita* whose family rancho was "just over the hill." Maria Augustina Sais (or Saez), daughter of Juan Maria and Maria Dominga (Valenzuela) Sais, was born at the Presidio of San Francisco and baptized at the local mission. Her grandparents, Micaela and Justo Nazario Sais, came to Alta California in the vanguard of Mexico's colonization efforts, traveling from Mexico to Monterey with Juan Bautista de Anza's second expedition (1775–1776).

The need for a helpmate, the expectation of future heirs, and sometimes even love, encouraged foreigners, especially naturalized Mexicans, to marry local *señoritas*. In a speech General Vallejo gave on July 4, 1876, celebrating the 1823 founding of Sonoma Mission, he named thirteen foreigners who had settled the county in its early years including Cooper, Black, Dawson, and McIntosh. According to Vallejo, "all of these, except McIntosh, were married to *hijas del pais*" (daughters of the country). On May 19, 1844, Father Louis Aloysius Lootens married thirty-four-year-old James Black and sixteen-year-old Maria Augustina Sais at the same San Rafael church where Black had been baptized.[7]

The last Mexican governor of Alta California, Pio Pico, formally granted Black ownership of Rancho Cañada de Jonive on February 5, 1845. While living at Jonive, Black raised both cattle and a family. On April 24, Maria Augustina gave birth to a daughter, named for her mother but called by her middle name, Augustina. Three years after Augustina's birth, the Black family welcomed a son who lived two short months. Black doted on his surviving daughter, stroking her hands and calling her "my dear."

The year 1845 continued to be a busy year for the family. According to H. H. Bancroft, Black served as the *alcalde* (mayor) of San Rafael in 1845, responsible for registering land grants and cattle brands. Ranchers registered brands and ear cuts as a way to identify and recover stolen livestock. Old Mac performed the duties of *alcalde* for Sonoma in August 1846 where he recorded his own brand as a stylized "B." In 1849, now *alcalde* for San Rafael, Old Mac registered Black's brand, a modified "A," probably inspired by Black's affection for his four-year-old daughter, Augustina.

With a wife, daughter, and rapidly expanding assets, Black signed his first will on June 12, 1846. The document was witnessed by prominent pioneer men of Marin, including Irishman Jasper O'Farrell, best known today for surveying and laying out the street map of San Francisco. Black's, Old Mac's, and O'Farrell's affairs would be intertwined well into the future.

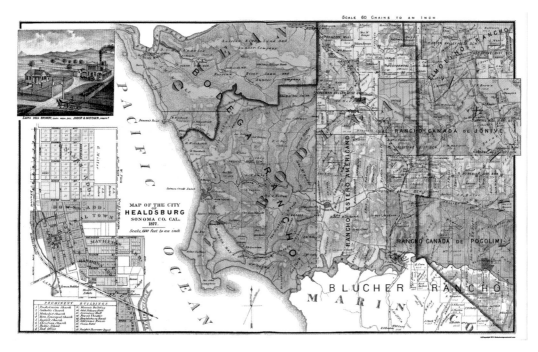

Black, McIntosh, and Dawson Ranchos. (@ 2011–2014 *www.mapsofthepast.com*)

Mission San Rafael. (*Marin History Museum*)

This is to Certify that this Day the the
first of May AD one Thousand eight hund
red and forty Nine James Black Presented
for Regestrey the Brand Vent and Ear
Mark as Disegnated in the Margin

Mark
3

Sinal

I therefore Manuel E McIntosh ist
Alcaldie of San Rafel by the Power
in me vested Do by these Presents
grant the Said James Black Sole
leave to Brand horses and Cattle
with the Said Disignated Marks
in the Distrect of San Rafel Done
the first day of May AD 1849
at my Office in San Rafel
                    Manuel E McIntosh
    ist Alcaldie Distrect of San Rafel

Black's registered brand. (*Marin History Museum*)

Jasper O'Farrell. (*Jack Mason Museum*)

Two years earlier, Old Mac had hired O'Farrell to survey his Rancho Estero Americano. O'Farrell must have liked what he saw since he leased the southern portion of the rancho from Old Mac in December 1847. The terms, effective while the old Scotsman lived, gave O'Farrell use of the farm, houses, mill, and all farming equipment. In turn, O'Farrell agreed to pay Old Mac $400 ($11,000) twice a year as well as providing regular provisions of fresh meat and "farm products." Old Mac retained the use of his house, a small portion of land, "one yoke of oxen, two milk cows and five tame horses." O'Farrell also sent 900 head of Old Mac's cattle to Black, a sizable herd whose number would reappear as a gift sixteen years into the future. After O'Farrell paid half of the first $400 installment, the payments stopped. Old Mac sued. Eventually, O'Farrell purchased the southern portion of Estero Americano outright for $5,000 ($156,000) in October 1851.

While O'Farrell negotiated his lease with Old Mac, he began to survey Rancho Nicasio, co-owned by Cooper and the prominent Mexican politician, Pablo de la Guerra. Documenting the irregular boundaries of the expansive Nicasio Rancho took O'Farrell two years, until September 1849. In the end, de la Guerra retained over 30,000 acres of Rancho Nicasio. Cooper claimed near 16,400 acres. O'Farrell's payment for survey services was slightly fewer than 9,500 acres.

Black's lust for land met its match in O'Farrell. In 1850, O'Farrell purchased the remaining northern portion of Rancho Estero Americano from Old Mac, making O'Farrell the sole owner of the original land grant. The next year, he traded his portion of Rancho Nicasio with James Black for full ownership of Rancho Cañada de Jonive, Black sweetening the deal with an additional $2,000 ($62,000). At this point, O'Farrell owned outright two original Mexican land grants totaling nine Spanish leagues or nearly 40,000 acres.

Black, and especially Maria, were pleased with the transition from Jonive to Nicasio. Black gained a foothold in prime grazing land for his longhorn cattle. Maria, closer to her brother, Don Domingo Sais, was well situated to resume family visits and multi-day fiestas at his Rancho Cañada de Herrera.[8] Black built a home for his family that eventually included seven rooms and an attic. A large spring located behind the house provided water during the county's inevitable drought periods. To the west, a 1,266-foot-high summit, still known as Black Mountain, stood between the family's homestead and the ocean, blocking coastal winds and mitigating the recurring fog.

After selling the last of his land grant to O'Farrell, Old Mac was left without a home, even one-half of a home. He moved in with Black and Maria, establishing a tradition that would last another twenty years. The two countrymen worked the Marin rancho, riding out with the *vaqueros* to round up the longhorn cattle, returning at night to the meal Maria had prepared. Finding his 17,000 acres too large for them to work on their own, Black portioned some land off in leases for six dairy ranches, often fully outfitted with rented cows. Marin and Sonoma dairymen were the envy of the country, reportedly producing in a good year, "sufficient milk to make on an average a pound of butter a day to each cow."

During the gold rush years, Black profitably drove cattle 130 miles north to the mines. Although cattle often lost weight or died in the process, gold-rich miners would pay many times what the San Francisco market could bear. The *Sonoma Democrat* (January

Black Mountain. (*Dewey Livingston*)

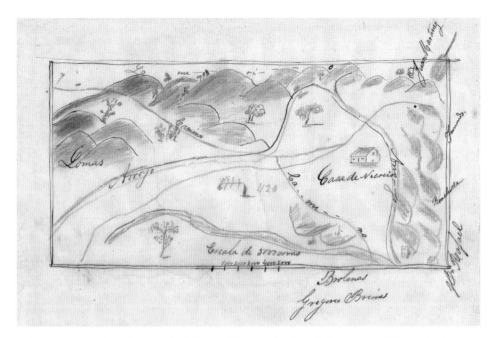

Above: Diseño of Black's Rancho Nicasio. Note the broken (lightning struck?) tree in the center of the map. (*California State Archives, Diseños Collection, Diseño 11543*)

Below: Rancho Nicasio, Black patent. Cropped. (*Anne T. Kent California Room, Marin County Free Library*)

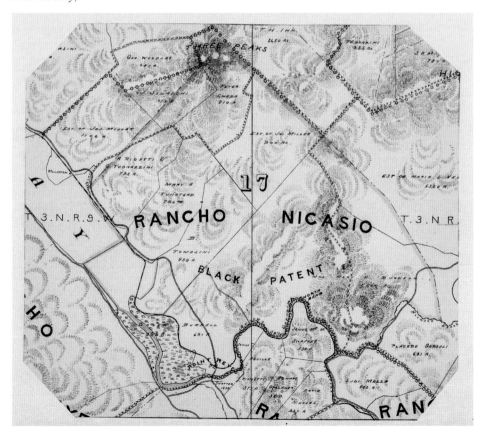

28, 1871) recalled Black's successes in the gold fields after which this "rugged Scottish lad found himself suddenly in possession of a wee bit [of] silver."

Without access to twentieth-century bridges, Black and his *vaqueros* typically drove his herds in a clockwise circle tracing the circumference of the San Francisco Bay to reach the city's cattle market. Historian Jack Mason recalled how once, determined to save miles and time, Black sent his herd across the ocean-facing waters of the Golden Gate. History does not record if Black chose incoming tide, outgoing tide, or the slack that was in between. Legend and logic report Black's cattle were not accomplished open-water swimmers. Bellowing and struggling, most of his four-footed wealth perished in the attempt.

Californians ratified the state constitution on November 13, 1849. The following September, President Millard Fillmore welcomed California as the thirty-first state—most critically, a slave-free state. In Marin County, the roster of wealthy and politically active men totaled only a few dozen white male voters. Black, like his contemporaries, held multiple Marin County positions including associate justice of the Court of Session (1850–1853), coroner, and county assessor (1852–1854).

With gold from livestock, hides, and dairy leases, Black continued buying thousands of acres of land, extending his holdings from bay to ocean: from San Pablo Bay to Point Reyes on the Pacific Ocean. The acquisition of Henry Halleck's Nicasio stake added the northern end of Nicasio Valley to Black's holdings.

In 1852, the same year San Quentin State Prison opened, Black spent $5,200 ($162,000) to purchase most of the 8,877-acre Rancho Olompali from Coast Miwok Indian Camillo Ynitia as a future wedding gift for then seven-year-old Augustina. In 1776, Camillo Ynitia's father, the last chief of his tribe, built the first adobe in Marin County and Ynitia constructed the second. A 1,558-foot-high bayside mountain also named Olompali (Miwok for "south village" or "south people") commanded the plain. Ynitia, the only indigenous Indian to receive and keep his tribe's land grant, lived on a 1,480-acre portion of his original land grant until his death in 1856.

Walter Skidmore, deputy assessor of Marin County, listed Black's property in 1853 as 8,857 acres in Nicasio, three lots in San Rafael, 7,380 acres at Olompali, tame horses, wild horses, mules, asses, six yoke of oxen, tame cattle, wild cattle, swine, fowl, mortgages, bonds, money due, growing crops, potatoes, grain, and locally printed currency or scrip. Unfortunately for the modern researcher, Skidmore did not value Black's extensive holdings.

Seasons changed. Wet winters gave way to daily cycles of blue sky and gray fog. Born in the spring, calves and foals soon abandoned their mothers' teats and learned to graze in fields of summer grass. Throughout, Black's evening whisky remained a constant. The 1860 United States census recorded Old Mac at eighty years old in residence with Black, his wife, and his daughter. Nine-year-old Lucy Smith, described as Augustina's cousin and Black's adopted daughter, completed the family. In a third will dated two years later, Old Mac left his property to the family who continued to give him shelter. The proceeds were "to be divided equally between them share and share alike."

On April 24, 1860, Augustina reached her fifteenth birthday, a milestone date in her mother's Mexican culture. Certainly, Black hosted a *fiesta de quinceaños* (fifteenth birthday party) for his daughter, complete with a rodeo and *fandango* dancing. The earliest photograph of Augustina to survive, perhaps taken for her special birthday,

Marin Cattle Ranch, *c.* 1860. (*Courtesy of the University of Southern California Libraries & California Historical Society*)

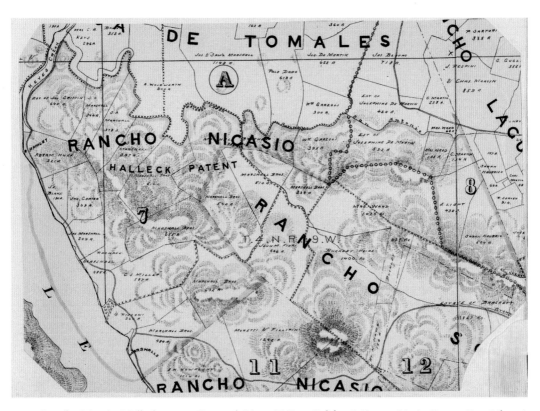

Rancho Nicasio, Halleck patent. Cropped. (*Anne T. Kent California Room, Marin County Free Library*)

Young Augustina Black. (*Marin History Museum*)

Marin, *c.* 1860. (*USC Digital Library. California Historical Library Collection*)

shows a corseted, dark-haired young woman with an oval face and carefully curled hair. Her pearl earrings, possibly a birthday gift from her father, reappear in photographs throughout her life and might be the "two pearl earrings" later willed to a granddaughter.

Afforded all the benefits of mid-nineteenth-century California wealth, Augustina wore the latest fashions and attended boarding school at the Convent of Notre Dame in San Jose, 100 miles to the south. The July 18, 1853, *Alta California* reported Augusta [*sic.*] Black received "Primary Class" awards for her good conduct, diligence, reading, writing, geography, and (to warm her mother's heart) catechism. A friend observed how Black treated his daughter "kindly and affectionately as good fathers do." On breaks from boarding school, Augustina returned to her parents' isolated home. By the time his daughter was of marrying age, Black was among the richest men in Marin County measured by land, commerce, gold, and paper scrip. Single men of marrying age regularly rode up the dusty lane to the Black home to court the dark heiress of one of Marin's wealthiest pioneers.

5

Augustina Comes of Age

Galen Burdell was born to James and Sila Burdell near Watertown, New York, on June 26, 1828. As is common for nineteenth-century records, Galen's birth date varies depending on the source you consult. Fortunately, Galen documented the particulars of his birth and arrival in California in his own hand for his induction as a member of the Society of California Pioneers in 1854.

As a fifteen-year-old, Galen apprenticed to his dentist uncles: John and Harvey Burdell. The *New York City Directory* for 1831–1847 lists Dr. Galen Burdell's dental office at the corner of Franklin and Broadway in lower Manhattan. Some said that Uncle Harvey, described by the *Alta California* newspaper (January 2, 1870) as "the meanest vagabond in New York," drove his nephew out of the city so Galen would not steal his patients. Others believed Galen left New York City to visit an uncle in Brazil. Regardless of his reason, Galen departed Baggs' Harbor, Boston (February 1849), as ship's surgeon aboard the *Duxbury*. According to a fellow passenger's diary, the 15,000-mile sea voyage to California was notable for the ship's sparse and unappetizing rations, including boiled rice and molasses as well as pork served in a monotonous rotation with beans, peas, and potatoes.

On May 24, the ship and her nearly one hundred passengers rounded Cape Horn. After seven months treating seasickness, measles, and injuries from the occasional fistfight, Galen arrived off San Francisco on August 21, 1849, in a seasonally dense summer fog. Seeking the coastal gap known as the Golden Gate, the *Duxbury* ran aground north of its goal, on a reef known today as "Duxbury Point." At high tide the following day, the ship limped into the San Francisco Bay, threading its way among the roughly 200 ships abandoned when their crews deserted to mine for "gold in them thar hills."

From 1849 to 1850, the population of San Francisco grew from less than 1,000 adult males to over 20,000 adults, including a few adventurous and profit-minded women. To serve the burgeoning population, Galen advertised his dental practice in the *Alta California* (September 6, 1849): "Copartnership—The undersigned have this day entered into copartnership under the firm of Thompson & Burdell for the practice of Dentistry. J. Whitlock Thompson and Galen Burdell M. D. Office on Clay Street." The new partners helpfully noted that their dental practice was located "next door to Woodruff & Addison Jewelry."

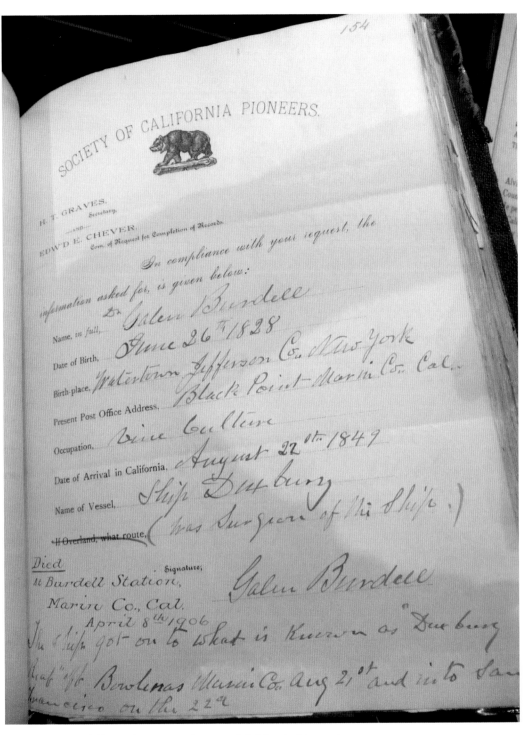

Galen Burdell member roster. (*Society of California Pioneers*)

The Best Chance Yet, for
CALIFORNIA!
Passage $125....To Sail Feb. 1st.

The Superior, Fast Sailing, Newly Coppered

SHIP DUXBURY,
Wm. C. VARINA, Master,

Will sail as above, from the North side of Union Wharf.
This Ship will take out a House and Store for the use of the Passengers there, free of charge for one month after arrival. Those wishing to take their families with them will improve this opportunity, as she will have a

Cabin fitted up expressly for Ladies!

A Regular Physician goes out in the Ship.
Six or eight Passengers can be taken forward at $100.
For Freight or Passage apply to

CHAS. H. COFFIN,
13 Dock Square, corner of Elm Street, Boston.

The fine Barque "CARTHAGE" will succeed the DUX-BURY, to Sail on the 20th of February. For Freight or Passage apply as above.

Propeller Power Presses, 142 Washington St., Boston.

(Propeller Power Presses, Ship Duxbury for California, 1849, woodblock print, 19 5/8 × 13 5/8 inches (49.848 × 34.608 cm), Peabody Essex Museum, gift of the Bostonian Society, 1957, M9577. Courtesy of Peabody Essex Museum. Photo by Barbara Kennedy)

Above: San Francisco Bay, June 1849. (*USC Digital Library. California Historical Library Collection*)

Right: Galen Burdell, *c.* 1849. (*Marin History Museum*)

Galen became an active member of San Francisco's business community, joining the St. Francis Hook and Ladder Company No. 1, a social and beneficial organization. When a scheme to get rich in Oregon failed, Galen and his two co-investors lost their entire capital of $1,000 ($30,000).

While Galen established his dental practice, the gold boom faded, leaving the 30,000 citizens of San Francisco to awaken from their ore-fueled excesses with a collective hangover. Dry goods and provisions shops stood empty for lack of patrons while the drinking dens, brothels, and gambling halls served boisterous and odorous crowds. Inept, if not outright corrupt, police, politicians, and judges scammed both the criminals and the citizens in order to fill their own pockets. Mayor John W. Geary acknowledged the city's porous justice system, citing how the city lacked "the means of confining a prisoner for an hour."

The notorious Sydney Ducks, roving gangs of "reformed" Australian convicts drawn to California's gold, were suspected of setting the city's tinder-dry wooden buildings ablaze in support of the incendiary trio—blackmail, arson, and looting. For good reason, lawless San Francisco gave birth to the term "hoodlum."

Fires, most criminally set, continued unabated for years. Three fires charred the city in 1849. The next year, San Francisco burned five times. Finally, on the night of May 3, 1851, yet another blaze began in a paint and upholstery store. By the time the inferno was beaten down to smoke and wet charcoal, flames had consumed eighteen blocks of the financial district including 1,500 to 2,000 buildings at a loss of $12,000,000 (nearly one-third of $1 billion in 2019).

The city's working class generally avoided the thugs, commenting after new reports of murder and mayhem, "the Sydney Ducks are cackling in the pond." In contrast, the city's shop owners, wholesalers, and professional men found themselves active targets of the Ducks' extortion and robberies. Finally galvanized into action, San Francisco's leading men then moved beyond merely grumbling and moaning in their drawing rooms and fancy-lady parlors.

On the evening of June 10, 1851, 103 men signed a hastily drafted constitution of the Committee of Vigilance, establishing nightly safety patrols and committing to deport felons. Later that same night, committee members twenty-five and seventy-two encountered a mob soundly beating John Jenkins, a Sydney Duck, for the theft of $1,000 ($30,000). The committee members rescued Jenkins from the mob, returning with their prisoner to the committee's meeting rooms. After slight deliberation and eschewing the niceties of jurisprudence, the committee hung Jenkins at the corner of Clay and Kearny Streets at 2.10 a.m., leaving him to swing for five hours.

The public, preachers, and eventually the police supported the committee's actions. On June 16, the *Alta California* applauded, "there has scarce been a robbery since" the committee's inception. Committee membership doubled, then tripled, finally ending at 710 members with Dr. Galen Burdell signed on as member number 259. By July, so many criminals had left the city that the nighttime patrols were abandoned. On September 15, the committee reorganized as an oversight, rather than active, organization. Their efforts had been prodigious. In 100 days, they had completed ninety-one arrests, resulting in one whipping, four hangings, fifteen criminals remanded to the authorities, and twenty-eight miscreants driven from California. Their work, or at least their energy, was spent—for a time.

San Francisco on fire, 1851. (*North Wind Picture Archives/Alamy Stock Photo*)

Hanging of John Jenkins. (*Courtesy of the California History Room, California State Library, Sacramento, California*)

Five years later, in the spring of 1856, San Francisco's criminals turned from arson and looting to more genteel political abuses, including voter fraud. Their new weapon was a technical achievement: "ballot-boxes, with false sides and bottoms, so prepared that by means of a spring or slide, spurious tickets … could be mingled with genuine votes." The reported ballot-box-stuffing mastermind was James P. Casey, editor of the *Evening Bulletin* newspaper. A beneficiary of fraud as well as its leader, Casey won a seat on the board of supervisors in a district where he was not even a candidate. Re-enter the Committee of Vigilance. Their new goals, as reported in the *Alta California* (August 27, 1856), included the eventual "execution of a few assassins, the banishment of a few score of noted criminals, and the voluntary expatriation of many others." Dr. Galen Burdell received a formal summons to participate in a committee hearing.

Late that summer, the executive committee ordered their rank and file to adjourn. Thirty years later, historian Josiah Royce observed after the dissolution of the second committee, "And thenceforth, for years, San Francisco was one of the best-governed municipalities in the United States."

In addition to his civic responsibilities, Galen's 1863 income of $3,000 ($63,000) from his dental practice, tooth-wash powder, and investments in toll roads and mines made him a viable suitor for Augustina's hand.

Reportedly, Galen and Augustina met in 1861 while she still attended school. After six months of correspondence between the young couple, with her father as their intermediary, Galen asked Black for his daughter's hand.

Years later, Augustina reflected on her parents' reactions to Galen's proposal. Her mother, Augustina recalled, was "very much in favor" of the marriage. After confirming his daughter shared Galen's affections, Black appraised the dentist as he might evaluate a bull or stallion. "Dr. Burdell is a gentleman of good standing in the community," Black said. Yet Galen was not a farmer—a professional flaw in Black's eyes. Eventually, Black approved of the marriage on two conditions: Augustina must finish school and she must wait until she was eighteen to marry.

Prior to her wedding, Black took Augustina to San Francisco to purchase her trousseau. Out of his element, Black must have shifted from foot to foot or sat bolt upright in an overstuffed chair, while his daughter fingered silk undergarments, considered china, and tried on hats. Deprived of a needed drink while in the posh store, he likely wished the glassware she held to the light contained an inch or two of whisky.

On October 1, 1863, thirty-six-year-old Dr. Galen Burdell of San Francisco checked into San Rafael's Marin Hotel.

Five days later, Galen and Augustina, at the promised age of eighteen, married at her parents' home. Augustina's wedding gifts included the 7,380 acres of Rancho Olompali her father had purchased for her eleven years earlier, as well as 900 head of his finest cattle. Handing her the deed to Olompali, Black promised, "There will be more coming to you, my dear, it is all in black and white." Augustina later reflected that by "black and white," she believed her father had made provisions for her in his will.

In a photo taken in late 1863 or early 1864, Augustina wears a wedding band as well as her *quinceaños* pearl earrings. Galen's absence might be explained by his remaining at their home in San Francisco to continue practicing dentistry. Her waist cinched stylishly tight, Augustina stands tall beside her diminutive parents. Her mother's generous curves contrast with her father's shrunken appearance. His balding head and deeply etched

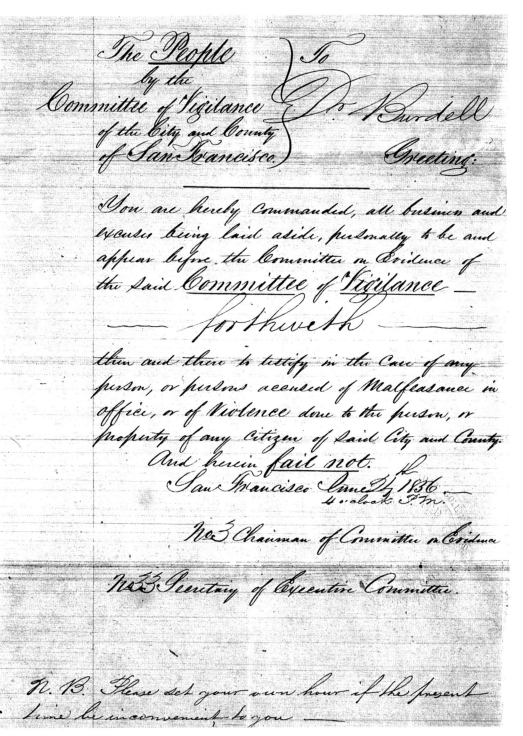

Committee of Vigilance summons, 1856. (*Burdell-Black family papers, BANC MSS C-B 952 Part II,*
The Bancroft Library, University of California, Berkeley)

Maria Augustina Black. (*John C. Bentiz*)

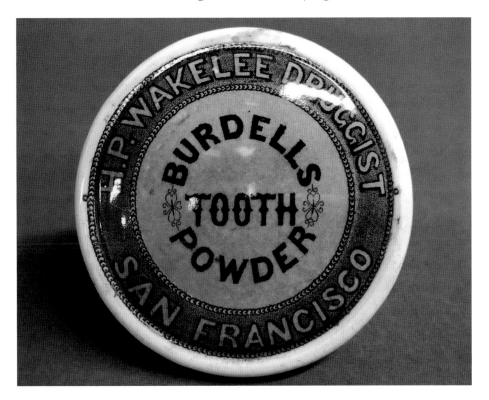

Above: Burdell tooth powder. (*Marin History Museum*)

Right: Galen Burdell. (*Marin History Museum*)

Marin Hotel. (*The Miriam and Ira D. Wallach Division of Art, Prints and Photographs: Photography Collection, The New York Public Library. (1865–1872). Marin Hotel, San Rafael. Retrieved from http://digitalcollections.nypl.org/items/510d47e0-2d41-a3d9-e040-e00a18064a99*)

The Black family. (*Marin History Museum*)

James and Maria Augustina (Sais) Black. (*John C. Benitz*)

face gave him the countenance of a winter-dried apple. Years of riding horseback across the rancho in sun, wind, and storm could mark a man's face, as could the tumblers of whisky Black regularly consumed.

This is the only photo of the family together.

Their clothing suggests James and Maria Augustina Black sat for their dual photographs the same day as their family portrait. In his photograph, Black appears kindly, less haggard than in the family group. The dark shadows under his round cheeks become rosy or perhaps flushed. Comparing these two photographs, we see the duality in the man: a gentle, loving father who too soon becomes a bitter, habitual drunk.

6
It Began With a Toothache

The constant throbs and random stabs of pain from toothaches demand that something—anything—be done for relief. On February 23, 1864, Augustina's mother, encased in a black taffeta dress, left Rancho Nicasio for treatment by her son-in-law of four months. To reach the respected Dr. Burdell, she endured a 20-mile buggy ride followed by a 40-mile rolling steamer trip, enveloped in the reek of the ship's cargo of poultry, hogs, and cattle.

Just hours after she arrived in San Francisco, Maria was no longer in pain.

She had died in Galen's dental chair.

Two days later, under the heading "DIED," the *Alta California* reported, "at the residence of her son-in-law, Dr. Galen Burdell, suddenly, of organic disease of the heart, [Maria] Augustina Black, wife of James Black, of Marin County, aged 36 years." Maria's remains returned home on the same steamer that had transported her to her death.

Later analysis suggested Maria had not died of "organic disease of the heart" but of accidental chloroform poisoning, an anesthetic in wide use since the 1850s. On the day Maria died, chloroform spared civil war soldiers the agony of battlefield amputations, although doctors found the compound tricky to administer. Death by overdose was not uncommon.

Less than a month later, the *Marin County Journal* (March 5, 1864) celebrated the formation of a Division of the Sons of Temperance—"one of the most significant occurrences that has taken place in San Rafael in the past fifteen years." Black took little note of the local opportunity to embrace sobriety. Bereft and furious at his wife's death, his drinking escalated. Tumblers of amber-colored liquor became bottles until finally, he kept a keg of whisky beside his bed.

Before he fully lost himself in drink, Black rewrote his will, leaving everything to Augustina. Still harboring his grudge, he instructed his attorney to not identify Augustina as the wife of Dr. Burdell. Assured by his lawyer that Dr. Burdell's name was merely a formality, that the dentist would not receive any property, Black insisted, "I don't want his name in my will."

When sober enough to remain upright, Black occasionally retraced his wife's last journey and visited Augustina in San Francisco. He seldom stayed the night, returning

Petaluma Steamer, *c*. 1860–1870. (*Society of California Pioneers*)

on the last boat to Petaluma. Augustina had seen her father drink. She had seen him drunk, but she was stunned when her normally stoic father "wept at our house."

Augustina, in turn, trekked north to Rancho Nicasio most Saturdays, sleeping in her mother's bed, in a room her father no longer entered. Weekend visits became weeklong stays. Occasionally, Augustina stayed in the old adobe homestead at Rancho Olompali, on the land her father had purchased as her wedding portion. To better care for her father, Augustina and Galen moved into Black's house from May through September 1864. It is hard to imagine more uncomfortable living companions than an inebriated Black and the man who killed his beloved wife.

Black's resident niece, brought from Wales to tend for her uncle, remembered him during this period as "forgetful, pacing the floor and picking at his meals." Neighbors described Black's immersion in drink: how his once shrewd and profitable business judgment began to fail, how he ejected paying tenants, and sold the same cattle twice. Once, he ordered a rodeo and forgot to attend the festivities. On jury duty, he slept through the arguments.

Black's cook recalled how his boss "was in the habit of drinking in the morning before dressing himself and continued drinking until the night. He would sometimes drink seven or eight times before breakfast, the quantity depending upon the amount of liquor he had aboard the night before." Stashing a 32-gallon barrel of whisky in one's bedroom does facilitate pre-breakfast tipples. The question of when breakfast occurred deserves some discussion. In the months after his wife died, Black would often remain in bed until suppertime, wishing his family and neighbors "good morning" as the sun began to set.

After Augustina returned to San Francisco, it is unclear if she knew how her father deteriorated. Galen took advantage of their time back in the city to participate in the

52

Mechanics' Institute's Fifth Industrial Fair in August 1865. Although the exhibits were not yet complete, the first day's attendance exceeded 4,000. Businessmen and courting couples promenaded the exhibit floor feasting on oysters and ice cream, listening to bands, and ogling the steam machinery, billiard tables, fancy needlework, guns, penmanship, manufactured glass, India rubber, as well as an exhibit on dentistry and dental chairs hosted by Galen and five fellow dentists. A dental chair on display, with "a very elegant spittoon" for the collection of silver and gold filings, impressed the judges sufficiently that it won a silver medal.

On August 6, 1866, President Robert J. Tiffany inducted James Black and seventeen other men into the Society of California Pioneers. Although other names preceded his in the alphabet, Black's name topped the list, suggesting first place was reserved for the oldest, sickest, or richest pioneer. As Black had been in California since 1832, it seems odd that his invitation to membership had taken so long. Perhaps word of his deteriorating condition had reached the membership committee who determined to solicit one of Marin's earliest pioneers—while he still lived.

On Christmas Eve that year, nearly three years after her mother's death, Augustina and Galen left San Francisco and her mother's hovering ghost, relocating permanently to Augustina's property at Rancho Olompali. Galen's leather desk chair moved from his city office to his rural study.

The couple's hoped-for sedate country life would last a mere two weeks.

REPORT

OF THE

Fifth Industrial Exhibition

OF THE

MECHANICS' INSTITUTE

OF THE CITY OF SAN FRANCISCO,

HELD AT THE PAVILION OF THE INSTITUTE,

From the 10th of August to the 9th of September,

A. D. 1865.

SAN FRANCISCO:

MINING AND SCIENTIFIC PRESS BOOK AND JOB PRINTING OFFICE.

No. 505 Clay Street, corner of Sansome.

1865.

Mechanics' Institute Fifth Industrial Fair, August 1865. (*Mechanics' Institute, San Francisco, California/archive.org*)

Galen Burdell's office chair. (*Marin History Museum*)

7

Too Drunk to Know

In 1851, in need of a third wife, Black's neighbor, Ignacio Pacheco, married twenty-four-year-old Maria Loretta Duarte, a younger sister of his second wife. Black, a witness to the wedding, regularly enjoyed the Pachecos' hospitality at their 6,680-acre Rancho San José, 20 miles east of Black's Rancho Nicasio. Ignacio died on November 29, 1864, nine months after Black's wife exhaled her last breath in Galen's dental chair.

The new widow cared for four sons, two daughters, and two stepchildren on a barely sustainable one-third portion of the original rancho. After both of their spouses died, Black, godfather to three of the widow's children, continued to call on Maria Loretta. In need of comfort, the grieving couple may have shared more than tea and sympathy. In late 1865, Maria Loretta informed fifty-five-year-old Black that she was pregnant.

On New Year's Day, 1866, Augustina, Galen, and Black's Welsh niece celebrated his birthday with turkey and side dishes followed, most likely, by whisky. A few days later, Augustina and Galen left for the old adobe at Olompali. On January 16, Black married Maria Loretta Duarte Pacheco, seventeen years his junior. That Augustina was 20 miles north during her father's wedding was of little importance—she was not invited. Neither was the niece taking care of Black nor Old Mac, who was once again in residence at Nicasio. Black sobered up enough to obtain dispensation from Father Lootens to marry the mother of his godchildren. In the first of many regrets, Black was later, in his own word, "ashamed" that he did not invite his daughter, niece, and companion of nearly forty years to his wedding.

A friend visited Black shortly after the ceremony. "I learn you have got married," he said. "I didn't know about it."

"I didn't know it myself until the day after, I was so drunk," Black replied, adding that his friend should never marry, lest he find himself with a bad-tempered wife.

Black's niece gathered her courage to confront her uncle. "Why was I not invited to your wedding?"

"There were no women present," he replied, an unlikely statement as the bride's daughters certainly attended.

His niece challenged him again. She had heard "a change was coming to the Pacheco family," referring to Maria Loretta's forthcoming child.

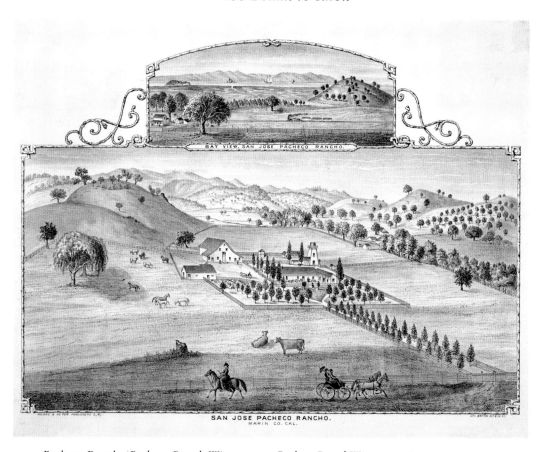

Pacheco Ranch. (*Pacheco Ranch Winery www.PachecoRanchWinery.com*)

"No, by God!" Black snapped. "She deceived me and she shall never get more than the law allows her." Apparently, Maria Loretta's pregnancy was no more, if it had ever been.

McIntosh had hunted with, lived with, and drank with Black for forty years before Maria Loretta tossed him out of Black's Nicasio home like the contents of last night's chamber pot. Old Mac was not the only one evicted by the change of wife. Black's niece reported she had been put off the ranch "in the dead of winter without a cent in my pocket."

If the new Mrs. Black had married for money, she had chosen her husband well. In the first year of their marriage, Black's federal tax payments, $335 ($5,000) placed him as the fifth wealthiest man in Marin and Sonoma counties. Two years later, his reported tax burden of $12,649 ($246,000) made him the most taxed, and therefore richest, man in the county. It is a puzzle why Black's taxes went up thirty-seven times over the intervening two years. Perhaps his cattle ranching had a particularly good year. Another interpretation, although speculative and unkind to Mrs. Pacheco Black, suggests she encouraged her husband to liquidate some of his land. After all, she had a clan of children to feed, the Pacheco rancho to maintain, and two daughters to marry off.

On March 22, 1866, two months after his wedding, Black drafted a third will leaving the greatest portion of his $750,000 ($15,000,000) estate to his new family. As for Augustina, the will stated that Rancho Olompali was her only legacy. She would receive nothing more.

Black's few bequests may have been examples of his damaged memory. On one hand, a trusted servant, Thomas Wood, received 950 acres plus related equipment, from which Wood was to pay Old Mac $20 ($354) every month in United States gold coins. Apparently, no amount of liquor could erase more than forty years of friendship.

On the other hand, Black left $3,000 ($53,000) each to his two sisters (Margaret and Jane) and 1,000 acres of land to his niece. Oddly, the will records that he did not know where his sisters and niece lived and assigns the money and property to Maria Loretta, should they not be located. Yet the niece taking care of Black, the one he sent for in 1865, was the same niece named in the will. The sisters' whereabouts were well known. Black could read but wrote with difficulty, so Augustina wrote letters to Jane for her father, and his niece remained in contact with her mother, Margaret. Continuing the questionable bequests, Black did not even own half of the property he left to an old friend.

Another extraordinary provision is the autonomy given to the will's executors: the full right to sell any of the estate's lands without supervision and without putting up any bonds or security. It is worth noting that some of the executors had little means or property of their own, and that Daniel Taylor, the county clerk of Marin County, drafted the will that made him an executor.

While his will reflected a legal reality, Black's personal moments were affectionate and generous. A neighbor questioned him about the will. "Mr. Black, they say you are not going to leave your daughter anything?"

"By God, I would give her my heart's blood. I can't help the talk; that is not so." Tears rolling down his cheeks, Black caught the neighbor around the shoulder, slapped him on

James Black's will, March 6, 1866. (*Anne T. Kent California Room, Marin County Free Library*)

the back, declaring his need for his daughter's affection. "Her mother's garden is going to rack and ruin. Augustina should care for both of us."

From her home at Olompali, Augustina regularly visited her father at Rancho Nicasio. Occasionally, she traveled to the Pacheco rancho to see him, where she found her stepmother "cool and distant." Alone in the Pacheco parlor, her father would stroke her hand, as he always did, and talk of happier days. When Maria Loretta came into the room, however, he would turn his face to the wall. Black eventually asked Augustina to only visit him in Nicasio. Her trips to the Pacheco residence "caused trouble."

Black's visits to Augustina's Olompali Ranch could be tragic and humiliating. One friend recalled how Black "lay on the ground drunk at Dr. Burdell's ranch, with his coat and shoes off, and rolled along the ground, muttering and chattering like an idiot." On another visit to Augustina, Black and a traveling companion stopped for whisky "and then some more whisky." At the Burdell's, they "drank whisky two or three times." Black spent time alone in the house with his daughter, leaving her side in tears. "That daughter of mine is a true lady," he told his companion. "I shall never forget her." On the way home, they stopped for yet more drinks.

Once, a muddled Black accused his daughter of betraying his wedding gift by transferring the deed to Olompali to Galen. Augustina denied the accusation and demanded to know who had slandered her. "A lady," her father replied, leaving Augustina to suspect the new Mrs. Black. When she questioned the "lady's" character and offered to deed the ranch back to her father, he declined. "No, my dear. I gave you that ranch."

One morning at the Pacheco rancho, Black woke a resident tenant, demanding the man find him something to drink. When the tenant returned to the rancho's sitting room, Black lifted the pint bottle to his lips, froze at the rustling of a lady's dress, then hid the bottle within his coat, leaving the tenant to conclude Black was afraid to drink in his wife's house.

Once, Black sat on a log with a friend, sharing his troubles in an atypically extended monolog:

> I'd rather be in hell than to have ever seen the Pacheco family. The children do not treat me well. I am not respected. I'm sorry to have brought Old Mac here. I offered her $22,000 ($398,000) to let me return to Nicasio but she won't take it. I'll not cover her back in silk out of my money. She'll get what the law allows and no more.

Ill at his ranch, Black confronted Maria Loretta. "Why don't you go home and take care of your family?" Black demanded, adding "I have people to care for me." Confident on his own land, he continued, "I may stay here—never return to your homestead." Relenting, he offered a compromise. "You can live with me. Your children—never."

When Augustina and Galen traveled east to visit his family, Black, presumably drunk, did not see her off. Crushed with regret, he cried to his niece, "Oh, my child, my child, she is gone from me!"

Hygiene, never a priority for Black, deteriorated. A tenant described how Black's bed in Nicasio "used to be in a filthy condition every morning. He was just like a child."

In the summer of 1869, Marin's weather reflected the area's Mediterranean climate. Fog cooled the mornings, retreated to the sea under the midday sun, and crawled ashore in the afternoon. Black spent the warmer months drunk—perhaps more drunk than usual, if such a thing was even possible. Black "swayed in his saddle like a ship at sea" a neighbor recalled, as if he stood the deck of a storm-tossed vessel. That July, Black pitched forward in his saddle, unsuccessfully grabbed leather for balance, and tumbled to the dirt, landing on a rock large enough to bend a plow. Keeling over was not a new maneuver for Black, but this time he suffered a grievous two-inch long and equally deep wound at the base of his skull. A section of bone went missing. Afterward, Black complained about how his head "kept jumping up and down." His agent described how his boss became "perfectly crazy for liquor," how he would repeat himself and "talk at random."

Black rallied sufficiently to visit his pregnant daughter in her confinement at the Lick House Hotel in San Francisco, close to her doctor and hospital should they be needed for her upcoming delivery. He refused the dinner she ordered for him.

"If you do not eat when you drink very hard you cannot expect to see many of your grandchildren," she admonished.

"They would be better off when I am dead," he replied.

Black's first grandchild, James Black Burdell, was born November 18, 1869.

When Augustina was able to travel, she visited her father at the Pacheco house. Before he finished reading a letter she had brought him, he heard someone coming and hid it under his arm. "Where is Mrs. Black?" he asked the servant girl.

"Lying down, sir."

He took Augustina in his arms. "My dear, you must leave this place, the women always make it worse for me."

Somehow, the addled Black managed a June 1870 trip to Olompali to see Old Mac. Once again, the two men must have sat with a wee dram of whisky in hand. In Monterey, nearly forty years before, they had planned their future. At Olompali, perhaps they reviewed their past. Friendship, wealth, love, loss, and the indignities of old age and decades of drinking likely flowed through their conversation as they reminisced.

On June 17, Black died at the Pacheco rancho in tremendous convulsions, leading some to say he was poisoned. The doctors believed the spasms consistent with softening of the brain, the end game of alcoholism. Celebrated by the Society of California Pioneers for his "many manly qualities," Black was buried in Mt. Olivet Cemetery in San Rafael on June 20, 1870—in the least prestigious part of the graveyard. The cemetery's rich and well-connected Catholics were laid to rest near the front gate. The wealthiest man in Marin County was interred in the remotest possible spot, his grave now separated from a tire and brake store by a chain-link fence.

Too ill to attend Black's interment, Old Mac remained at Rancho Olompali. Perhaps Black's death reminded the elder Scot of the fragility of life. The next month, he signed his last will. With Black and his first wife deceased and Augustina living comfortably at Rancho Olompali, Old Mac's modest will included only two bequests.

First, he forgave any outstanding debts from his "old friend, John McIntosh," whose relationship to Old Mac remains unclear. Second, after paying his debts, the remaining $4,000 ($82,000) was invested in land for the benefit of Josefa Miranda, to whom he was "indebted for many acts of kindness." It is interesting to speculate what kindness Josefa offered Old Mac during his life. Josefa was married so it is unlikely the debt was

Black's grave in Mt. Olivet Cemetery, Corte Madera, California. (*Heather Powell*)

romantic. Whatever Old Mac's reasons, his generosity must have been appreciated—as Josefa went on to have twelve children.

Six weeks after his best friend died, Old Mac formally granted Galen the "full power and authority to do and perform all and every act and thing whatsoever requisite and necessary to be done." In short, Galen had complete control over all of Old Mac's affairs. The aging Scotsman signed over his estate with a thick hand: Manuel Edward McIntosh.

Old Mac died at Rancho Olompali on November 7, 1870, five months after Black. He was buried next to his lifelong friend, under a gravestone with blanks for his date of death and age—his name misspelled.

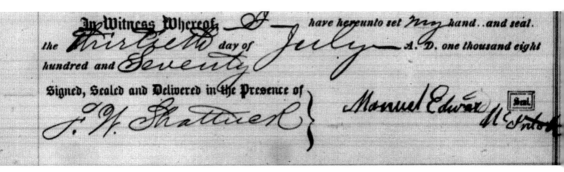

McIntosh's power of attorney. (*Burdell-Black family papers, BANC MSS C-B 952 Part II, The Bancroft Library, University of California, Berkeley*)

James Black's (left) and Old Mac's graves at Mt. Olivet Cemetery, Corte Madera, California. (*Heather Powell*)

8

One Trial After Another

Normally, after a burial, families have time to grieve before the legalities of probate begin. Unfortunately for Augustina, one of her father's executors needed to leave Marin county, rushing the proceedings. The morning after Black's burial, Augustina, Galen, and the three co-executors (Misters William Benitz, Upton M. Gordon, and Daniel T. Taylor) traveled to Rancho Nicasio to search for Black's private papers. Augustina waited outside in her carriage, either unable to visit her father's home so soon after his death or unwilling to face her stepmother who was inside. As an executor read the will to Maria Loretta, one of her stepsons translated his words into Spanish. Except for a scattering of nominal bequests, all of Black's land, money, and property had been left to her. The new widow Black was understandably "satisfied" with her late husband's generosity.

Galen needed no translation to understand that his wife had been denied any claim to her father's wealth. The next day, Mr. and Mrs. Benitz and Mr. Gordon arrived at the Marin Hotel to read the will to Augustina. Mr. Benitz departed, presumably for his out-of-the-county trip, leaving his wife, Josephine, behind as a witness. Gordon began to read, slowly and carefully enunciating each word. Impatient with his painstaking delivery, Augustina asked to read the will herself—as not to tax him. Forewarned by Galen, she scanned quickly, turning pages, referring backward, rereading, searching for—but never finding—her portion of her father's estate. During her frantic shuffling came the dry rasp of tearing paper.

"In God's name, Mrs. Burdell, what are you doing?" Gordon cried. Augustina dropped the will and fled.

Historian Jack Mason believed Augustina "tore her father's signature off in her teeth, apparently swallowing it." The *Marin Journal* (July 2, 1870) contended she tore the will in half or merely ripped his signature from the final page. On Christmas Day 1873, the same newspaper offered a different version of events, reporting that Augustina tore the will "in two, dividing the signature…in the hopes of getting one-half of the property"—a most Solomon-like gesture, if that story is true. Regardless of the actual destruction, Augustina's "mutilation" of her father's will birthed many inches, feet actually, of newspaper coverage. The sound of that will's tearing reverberated from the nineteenth into the twenty-first century as the inspiration for this book.

Gordon gathered the damaged papers and left the hotel "greatly excited." The co-executors took the defaced will to the Grand Jury, conveniently in session. On Monday, June 27, 1870, Augustina appeared in court and admitted her guilt, explaining her actions as "undue excitement, and that it was not her intention to injure, defraud, or render invalidate [*sic*] her father's will." Given that a copy of the will had been located, the district attorney, whether influenced by Augustina's distress or the future sporting doctrine of "no harm, no foul," ruled "*nolle prosequi*"—he would drop the case.

On July 20, 1870, five days before the probate judge was to accept Black's will, Augustina filed a protest contesting her father's will, demanding a jury trial. The document, she claimed, was not binding because her father was incapacitated by drink, unable to make sound decisions, and that Maria Loretta had exercised undue influence over her failing spouse.

In late August, the trial of Mrs. Burdell *v.* Mrs. Black began in Marin's spectator-packed adobe courthouse. Prominent Marin citizens appeared as jurors and witnesses, dividing the county into team Black and team Burdell. Newspapers, most notably the *Sonoma Democrat* (January 28, 1871), joined team Burdell, describing Maria Loretta as a "managing Mexican widow" and "the scheming widow Pacheco."

Augustina's side argued that her father was not himself. Alcohol and its resulting falls had addled his brain. Why else would a man not invite his beloved daughter, best friend, and favorite niece to his wedding? A neighbor testified how Black was much changed after the death of his first wife, that he had become fitful and erratic.

Executor Gordon agreed that Black drank heavily after the death of his first wife but "he would not transact business while drunk" and that he was "a man of commonsense." Maria Loretta testified, in Spanish, how Black was godfather to three of her children and had promised her that he would treat them "as if they were his own." Two neighbors certified Black was sober when he signed his will shortly after marrying the Widow Pacheco. A former county sheriff declared Black was "prompt" in paying his taxes.

After nearly two weeks of testimony, the case was handed to the jury around noon. Around dinner time, they reported themselves deadlocked at seven against the will (team Burdell) and five in favor of it (team Black). One hopes that justice, not hunger, was uppermost in their minds when they rendered their decision.

Strike one.

Maria Loretta was named administratrix of the Black estate until the matter of the will could be settled. As the months dragged on, one of the estate's dairy leases expired. She visited the vacated land only to find that Tom Wood had taken possession

THE SONOMA DEMOCRAT.

"THE WORLD IS GOVERNED TOO MUCH."

L. XIV.   SANTA ROSA, SONOMA COUNTY, CAL., JANUARY 28, 1871.   NO. 16.

Sonoma Democrat, January 28, 1871. (*California Digital Newspaper Collection, Center for Bibliographic Studies and Research, University of California, Riverside, www.cdnc.ucr.edu*)

of the ranch. After all, the land had been granted to him in Black's will. If the will was affirmed, Maria Loretta must relinquish the ranch. Maria Loretta conceded the ranch battle to Wood and concentrated on winning the estate war.

A second trial in front of Probate Judge Joseph Almy began on November 7, 1870. Echoing the first trial, the courtroom drama lasted two weeks. The jury never reached a decision.

Strike two.

A year later, almost to the day, Judge Almy struggled to gavel the third trial to a start. After the attorneys interviewed seventy-five potential jurors, the jury contained only eight men. It took another thirty-five or forty candidates (reports vary) to fill the remaining four seats. After the now typical two-week trial, the jury reported their decision: eight repudiated the will (team Burdell) and four insisted the will was valid (team Black)—another deadlock, despite one more juryman voting against the will. It seemed redwood trees reached maturity faster than the probate court reached a decision.

Strike three.

Fortunately for the scorned daughter, a court of law is not a baseball diamond. The judge did not call Augustina "out" and order her off the field. She was free to demand a legal decision as long as her ability to pay held out. Still, most believed "a fair and impartial trial" could not be found in Marin. Besides, the three trials had exhausted Marin's 400 potential jurymen. A new venue with an ample selection of unbiased jurors waited to Marin's south, across the waters of the Golden Gate: San Francisco.

Months passed. A new year debuted. Taxes came due.

The *Daily Alta California* (August 5, 1872) listed all taxpayers whose properties were valued at $20,000 or more. Galen Burdell's $160,523 ($3,500,000) assets more than doubled Maria L. Black's Pacheco property of $71,094 ($1,500,000). As administratrix of the Black estate, Maria Loretta also controlled Marin's largest holdings—$484,740 ($10,500,000). Her wealth (Black's wealth) allowed her to dress as she pleased, not in her late husband's feared silks but in plaid, when she posed for Bradley and Rulofson, the most sought-after photographers in San Francisco.

Two questionable characters, Candido Gutierres and Manuel Castro, whispered to Galen on November 12, 1873, that they could bring testimony to defeat Black's will. Eager for a speedy end to the stressful and expensive trials, Galen paid the men $250 ($5,000) with a guarantee of $5,000 ($108,000) when they produced the will-busting evidence. Later, unknown to Galen, the two men sold their contract to Lewis H. Bailey, who would resurrect Gutierres and Castro's unfulfilled claim well into the future.

On December 9, 1873, an inexplicable twenty months after Judge Almy ordered the trial moved, the Marin court transferred its trial papers to San Francisco. With an alacrity not seen in Marin, the fourth trial started a mere four months later on March 16, 1874, in front of probate Judge Myrick. Where the denizens of Marin and Sonoma counties watched the trials as concerned neighbors, the good citizens of San Francisco found the spectacle of two prominent women fighting over money and land intoxicating. The *San Francisco Evening Bulletin*, obliging the public's need for gossip, devoted lengthy daily columns to "The Great Black Will Case."

Hordes of witnesses supported both sides' assertions. As the *Marin Journal* reported, the trial "necessitates, loosely speaking, the attendance of half the population of the county." Nearly forty years before the Golden Gate Bridge opened, the ferries plying

Right: Maria Loretta Duarte
Pacheco Black, *c.* 1873.
(*Marin History Museum*)

*Below: San Francisco Evening
Bulletin*, March 1874. (*San
Francisco Public Library*)

THE GREAT BLACK WILL.

he Contest Resumed in the Probate Court for
the Fourth Time—Interesting Opening of the
Case by the Contestant's Counsel—Mr.
Campbell Tells the Other Side of the Story.

their way from Marin to San Francisco must have seen an impressive jump in ridership during the trial. One of those witnesses, the most respected Dr. Alfred W. Taliaferro, who treated Black during his fatal illness, was shot on March 3, two weeks before the trial started. Fortunately for everyone, especially for Dr. Taliaferro, he had recovered in time to testify.

Perhaps in evidence of the land in question, in 1874, well-known surveyor Hiram Austin submitted his plot of the full extent of James Black's Nicasio ranch.

Augustina maintained her position that her father was not of sound mind due to excessive drink and that his second wife had turned him against his daughter. Her lawyer also argued that Black had a "hereditary disposition to insanity. His sister Margaret ... had been insane for many years, produced by the sudden loss of her husband." The insanity charge might have represented legal piling-on but the similarity to Black's own situation was striking.

Augustina's lawyers used the will itself to prove Black's addled mind. Daniel T. Taylor, in his role of Marin County Clerk, had drawn up the will in which he was both a beneficiary and an executor with unhampered control to manage the estate until the youngest of Maria Loretta's children was twenty-five years old—eighteen long and potentially profitable years. That Taylor was even an executor was puzzling since he had frequently earned Black's wrath for his unpaid loans, all the while dressing in finery. Black had once lamented how the only way he could get value for the $1,500 ($30,000) that he had loaned to Taylor was by having the "harum-scarum" man write some documents for him.

Maria Loretta's team argued that even if Black was a habitual drunkard, he understood what he was doing when he signed the will. And as to undue influence on the part of the second Mrs. Black, "it is proper that the wife should have influence with her husband in the disposition of his property." In their final damning assertion, Maria Loretta's lawyer contended Black had left nothing to his daughter for fear that his land or money might line the pockets of a man he abhorred. On that last point, at least, team Black had truth on their side. Black had hated Galen with a passion not drowned but inflamed by whisky.

For three weeks, witnesses alternately described Black as a gentleman who never did business while drunk and as an intoxicated and bitter man, terrified of his wife. As the trial approached its third week, William Benitz, one of the will's three executors, requested the court to excuse him from his duties. Deep in preparations for his coming move to Argentina, Benitz may have been eager to put the interminable trials behind him or perhaps the weight of Augustina's lawyers' arguments converted him to the other side. Whatever his motivation, when it came to the executors, then there were two: Taylor, the fancy dresser who did not pay his bills, and Gordon, the banker who held the estate's money.

Finally, the charges and countercharges were exhausted. On April 2, 1874, Judge Myrick took a full ninety minutes to charge the jury prior to their deliberations. At 3 p.m., the jury left to deliberate the assigned ten issues relating to whether Black was of sound mind when he signed his will and if he was under undue influence by either people or alcohol.

At 8.45 p.m., nearly four years since the first hung jury, the San Francisco jury sided with Augustina on all ten counts. They could have returned a verdict in Augustina's

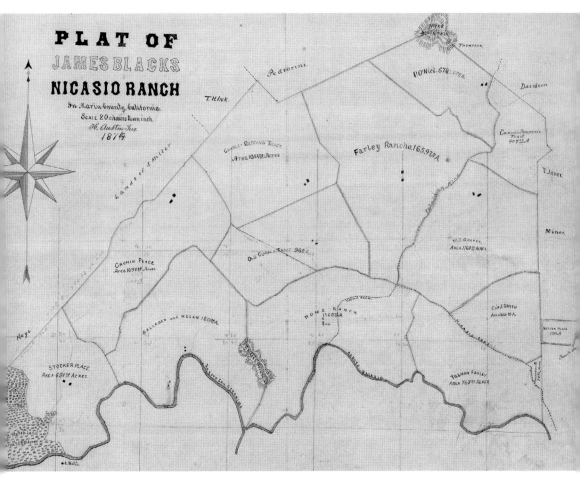

Black's rancho by Hiram Austin. (*Nicasio Historical Society*)

THE BLACK WILL CONTEST.

The Proponent's Case—Farther Testimony upon the Habits and Peculiarities of James Black.

San Francisco Evening Bulletin, March 1874. (*San Francisco Public Library*)

THE BLACK WILL CASE.

The Evidence Offered in Support of the Will—Witnesses Declare that Mr. Black Treated his Wife Kindly and was of Sound Mind.

San Francisco Evening Bulletin, March 25, 1874. (*San Francisco Public Library*)

William Benitz, 1868. (*John C. Benitz*)

70

favor in minutes, but the judge insisted they record a vote on each of the ten counts. In the end, Black's last will was declared invalid because he was deemed to be "habitually intemperate" and not of sound mind. The *San Francisco Chronicle* reported: "Under this Verdict, the estate will be equally divided between Mrs. Black and Mrs. Burdell—just as though the deceased died intestate."

Pleased that she did not have to wait eighteen years to be rid of the will's executors, Maria Loretta received Black's Nicasio home and its surrounding land. Augustina emerged vindicated and rich. She received 5,800 acres from the northwest portion of her father's vast holdings stretching to Point Reyes Station, including Black Mountain. Added to her own Olompali stake, she now owned over 10,000 acres of Marin county. No wonder Galen treated all who testified on his wife's behalf—and the jury—to a champagne dinner.

Augustina's win was satisfying—and expensive. The final trial totaled $40,000 ($916,000) in related charges. She received a mere $4,587.50 ($105,000) for expenses. The court denied payment to the executors of the discredited will, although Gordon did receive a modest $347 ($8,000) in witness fees and mileage payments. Prior to the trial, Augustina's three attorneys (James McMillian Shafter, J. M. Sewell, and Judge J. B. Southard) had each negotiated a contingent fee of one-eighth the value of Augustina's gains. The three men split roughly $100,000 ($2,300,000) for their successful efforts. Maria Loretta's unsuccessful legal team earned a total of $30,000 ($687,000).

Maria Loretta, it seemed, felt no pressure to share the estate to which she remained the sole administratrix. In November 1874, seven months after the judge's decision to set aside the will, Maria Loretta had yet to dispense any of the estate's assets. Augustina sued and the court ordered Maria Loretta to begin the distribution. Nearly one year after the conclusion of the fourth trial, a three-man commission, paid $1,230 ($29,000) for their work, recommended how the estate should be divided. *The Marin Journal,* March 25, 1875, reported their "work gives general satisfaction."

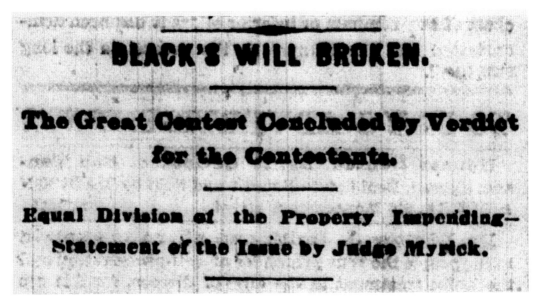

San Francisco Evening Bulletin, April 3, 1874. (San Francisco Public Library)

The July 27, 1876, *Marin Journal* listed tax assessments under the heading: "The Heavy Men of Marin County." A handful of women made the list, among them: Mrs. M. L. Black (Maria Loretta), as guardian of Pacheco minors; Mrs. M. A. Burdell (Augustina); and Mrs. M. L. Velasco—Maria Loretta had married again, for the third time. The Pacheco minors' assessments of $23,208 ($565,000) were dwarfed by Augustina's taxes of $210,655 ($5,100,000) and Maria Loretta's reported duties of $172,476 ($4,200,000). Of course, since Augustina had not yet received her share of her father's estate, that money most likely rested in Maria Loretta's bank account.

Four years later, the 1880 Federal Census reported Maria L. Velasco living on 4th Street in San Rafael with her new husband, Vicente (or Usidrio) Velasco, three Pacheco sons, and four servants. Thirty-nine-year-old Vicente, more than a decade younger than his wife, listed his occupation as "retired merchant." Marrying money does allow one to forego common commercial pursuits.

On Saturday, January 27, 1877, nearly three years after the judge and jury awarded her one-half of her father's estate, Augustina and Galen traveled to U. M. Gordon's Banking House in San Rafael. Gordon had been one of the three executors of the discredited will and a devoted member of team Black. That day, his hand must have trembled as he crossed out and rewrote the amount of $15,163.45 ($369,000) in United States gold coins. With neat Catholic-school-trained penmanship, Augustina signed the receipt. As witness, Galen added his name with a flourish.

With the trials concluded and the financials settled, the Burdells could try, once more, to retire to their Olompali estate.

The Heavy Men of Marin County.

We append a list of all the taxpayers of this county who are assessed $10,000 and upwards, with the amount of their assessments :

Allen, C. D.	$ 41,330
Alemany J. H., in charge for Cath. Church	30,680
Angellotti, G	14,690
Arner, Theodore Mrs.	23,400
Bloom, Jos. & Jas., in chge for H. Cowell	19,434
Bailey, Robt	12,898
Brackett, J. S.	39,202
Burbank, G. W	18,455
Bunn, Geo.	20,215
Bloom, Jas.	15,070
Brown, Wm.	18,015
Barnard, W. L.	10,820
Black, Mrs. M. L., as guardian of Pacheco minors	23,208
Bresson, Jos.	12,895
Barber, Wm	17,240
Burke, Wm	11,448
Burdell, Mrs. M. A	210,655
Brown, John Mc., Dalton, et al	84,619

Marin Journal, July 17, 1876. (*California Digital Newspaper Collection, Center for Bibliographic Studies and Research, University of California, Riverside, www.cdnc.ucr.edu*)

Maria Loretta Valesco and Vincente, her third husband. (*Marin History Museum*)

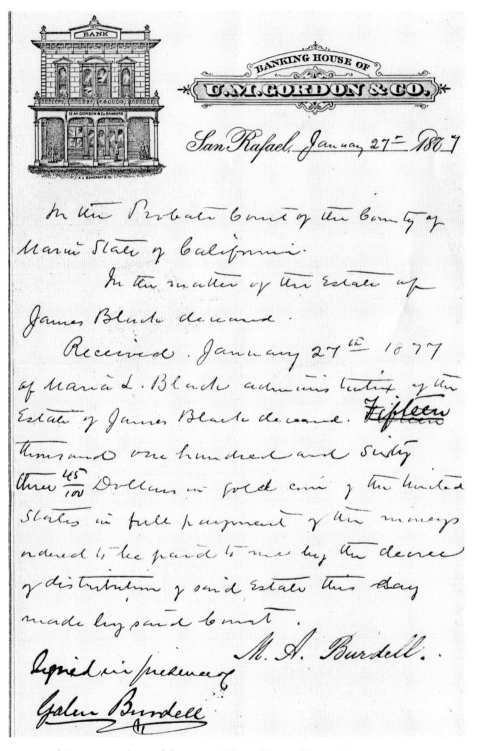

Receipt of Augustina's share of the estate. (*Marin History Museum*)

9

The Burdells of Olompali

Augustina and Galen returned to Olompali, down the home's avenue of oak, laurel, and imported trees.

They dismantled the original adobe built by Ynitia's father and recycled the bricks to add an extensive dining room to the now two-story home, which was updated with contemporary conveniences and luxurious furnishings. Wealthy and generous, the couple regularly shared their good fortune. At Christmas, a rancho wagon delivered turkeys to neighbors' homes. Galen went as far as to leave gold watches at the homes they visited when traveling back East.

In October 1874, Galen joined a commission of "75 to 100 of the most substantial and enterprising citizens of Sonoma and Marin counties, representing enough wealth to gridiron the district." The group's goal was to build a railroad from Petaluma to San Rafael, allowing connecting passengers to reach San Francisco in ninety minutes, for less than $0.75 ($30). Galen's pledge to participate in San Rafael's $100,000 ($2,300,000) contribution was not completely philanthropic. As one of the rallying speakers noted: "with a railroad from Petaluma to San Rafael, [the adjoining] lands will not only double and treble in value but increase ten-fold." Conveniently for the Burdell family pocketbook, the proposed train railway passed through Rancho Olompali.

With time and money, the Burdells traveled extensively. From Japan, Augustina brought home magnolias, oleanders, Japanese maples, and camellias—trees and shrubs now commonplace in Marin's gardens and parks. Mrs. George Boyd of San Rafael wrote, "to Mrs. Burdell belongs the distinction of building the first ambitious garden in the county. As a bride she commenced redesigning the grounds, grading in front of the house in long graceful terraces toward the bay."

The Olompali gardens followed a formal design, laid out beneath pines and eucalyptus, with brick paths radiating from a circular flower bed in front of the house. On the outer edge of the wheel was "the first planting of exotics in the county." A stately redwood tree stood in the garden, "grown it was said from a seed found in the crop of a quail killed at Fort Ross." Chinese laborers crafted mortarless stone walls defining the garden's perimeter. To this day, remnants of Augustina's palms, pomegranate hedges, and stone fountain delight those who tour the remains of their home.

Above: Driveway to Olompali. (*Marin History Museum*)

Below: Augustina and Galen Burdell. (*John C. Benitz*)

Rancho Olompali stone fountain and grotto, originally topped by a golden crane. (*Heather Powell*)

Rancho Olompali oaks and pomegranate hedges. (*Library of Congress/National Park Service*)

While his wife turned scrubland into a verdant garden, Galen managed Olompali's livestock, as well as the extensive Nicasio dairy ranches, a legacy from Black's original property. An inventory from 1900 illuminated the ranch's extensive holdings: 289 cows, including sixty-one heifers and an equal number of calves sired by the rancho's resident eight bulls; twenty-seven horses and three colts; 300 sheep; 1,700 chickens; and a pig colony of ten brood sows, seventy-five young piglets, and two very proud boars.

Among their other innovations, Augustina and Galen brought the first citrus trees to northern California, establishing an industry that grew to $3 billion in 2019, with some ranchers still harvesting citrus from trees planted by their grandparents. Olompali's 200 orange trees, representing twenty varieties, were said to rival those of Los Angeles. His fields held a cornucopia of fruit including apples, pears, quince, figs, pomegranates, persimmons, apricots, peaches, and plums. The Burdells' personal "Garden of Eden" did not extend to bananas, which struggled in Marin's Mediterranean climate.

In 1880, Olompali included a research vineyard with thirty varieties of grapes and an additional sixty acres of bearing vines. The grapevines must have been Galen's pride since he listed his occupation as "Wine Culture" in his official membership papers in the Society of California Pioneers.

A year after the fourth trial ended, with the estate settled and Gutierres and Castro's promised will-busting secret documents long forgotten, Bailey, the owner of Galen's original contract, sued for the promised $5,000 ($118,000). Burdell argued that the two men never produced any documents. In his eyes, no documents equaled no payment. Unfortunately for Galen, the jury agreed with Bailey, ordering Galen to pay the full $5,000 plus 10 percent interest. Thank goodness Augustina had her father's will declared invalid, yielding more than enough money to pay this questionable debt.

On March 21, 1876, a few weeks short of her thirty-first birthday, Augustina gave birth to a daughter, whose first name evolved over her lifetime from Maybell to Mabel to Mary. Her last name varied from Burdell to Coleman, to Smith, to Lichtenberg as she cycled through husbands. Maybell's childhood, if not her adulthood, must have been placid in comparison to her brother's early years. James Black Burdell, six years his sister's senior, had endured his grandfather's death and his parents' distraction with seemingly endless trials.

After the railroad reached Burdell's Station (then named Olema Station) in 1875 or 1876, Galen established a bar and hotel to serve the trains' passengers and crew members. Trains also brought friends to Olompali to meet the new baby and visit the family. In 1879, in defiance of her father's wishes, Augustina deeded Galen 950 acres surrounding the train depot. By the early 1880s, Olema Station included a hotel, saloon, railroad depot, blacksmith shop, stable, butcher shop, general store, and post office, as well as a dentist's office—not Galen's. In 1891, the town was renamed Point Reyes Station.

Galen extended his wife's land holdings by reclaiming the marshes near Mount Olompali, now renamed Mount Burdell. Galen and his neighbors set rows of pickets in bay mud. Over time, the trapped silt turned swamp into tillable land stretching four miles into the San Francisco Bay.

In early 1900, seeking relief from the grinding pain of gallstones, Augustina entered Lane Hospital in San Francisco, California. Whether from prudence or premonition, she dictated her will, which was signed by hospital witnesses. Shortly before undergoing

Olompali Vineyard looking south, *c.* 1898. (*Frank Kuykendall/John C. Bentiz*)

Early Point Reyes Station. (*Jack Mason Museum*)

Galen Burdell, age sixty. (*John C. Benitz*)

Rancho Olompali and Tidal Land. (*Anne T. Kent California Room, Marin County Free Library*)

surgery on January 23, 1900, Dr. William Fitch Chevey held her hand while she prayed, "Lord, unto thee I commend my spirit. Lord have mercy on me."

She died during the operation. Some blamed chloroform poisoning for her death, the same soporific that took her mother nearly forty years earlier. Augustina was fifty-four years old.

In the final accounting, Augustina's net worth included nearly $10,000 in cash ($310,000) and $400,000 ($12,000,000) in real and personal property. Cognizant of the drama and trauma that wills can often cause, Augustina had crafted her will clearly and fairly, dividing her estate among Galen and her two children while assigning $1,000 each ($30,000) to the three women who had testified most ardently on her behalf during the trials.

Neither were Augustina's grandchildren forgotten. Each received direct bequests, as well as later distributions. In one example, the contents of Rancho Olompali's main home were Galen's "to have, hold and enjoy" until his death, at which time the household goods (furniture, pictures, porcelain, china, silverware, and library) would go to a granddaughter. Another granddaughter would receive a pair of pearl earrings, most likely the jewelry often worn in Augustina's photographs. The will included an innovative provision to relieve Olompali's $135,000 ($4,200,000) mortgage. Before receiving their land, livestock, or physical property, legatees had to reduce

Augustina Black Burdell with pearl earrings. (*Marin History Museum*)

Mountain View Cemetery. (*Hank Chapot*)

the Bank of Sonoma loan with small payments in proportion to the value of their inheritance.

Augustina's funeral was held at Olompali. Her cremation at the Odd Fellows Cemetery Columbarium in San Francisco was witnessed by four men; Galen was not among them. In May, her ashes were transferred to Mountain View Columbarium in Oakland, California.

Six years later, on April 8, 1906, ten days before San Francisco's legendary earthquake, Galen died at seventy-eight years old. *The Marin Journal* noted his passing:

> For some days he has been sinking gradually and the end came quietly and without pain, the pioneer going peacefully to sleep, to wake no more on earth. The death of Dr. Burdell marks the going out of one of California's foremost pioneers—a man beloved and respected by all who knew him—and he was known to all.

Also cremated at the Odd Fellows Cemetery Columbarium, Galen joined his wife at the Mountain View Columbarium.

After Galen's death, his son, James, expanded his parents' home into a twenty-six-room mansion. Traded from hand to hand, the homestead underwent many transitions. In 1965, $150 bought a family membership at the Rancho Olompali Recreation and Swim

Galen Burdell in front of the fountain at Rancho Olompali. (*In Tamal Land, by Helen Bingham, Calkins Publishing House, San Francisco, CA, 1906*)

Grateful Dead at Olompali. (*Herb Greene*)

Club, located at the "site of the historic Burdell Mansion" bragged the club's marketing brochure. The following spring, the newly formed Grateful Dead turned on, tuned in, and dropped out at the mansion, returning through the late 1960s to host all-night jams.

When the 189-year-old building burned in February 1969, the wooden walls of the dining room slumped into smoldering ruins, revealing the bricks of Ynitia's original adobe among the ashes. The damaged home, outbuildings, and most of the original acreage were added to the Registry of Historic Places in early 1973 and became a California State Park in 1977. As of 2003, Charmaine Burdell, Augustina and Galen's granddaughter, still retained a few acres of her family's once county-spanning estate.

For most of the nineteenth century, through the skin trade, Russian incursions, gold fever, vigilantes, statehood, cattle ranching, dairy farming, and winemaking, James Black and his daughter Maria Augustina, much like the state of California, struggled, succeeded, failed, and rose again. Their experience, while unique in its particulars, shared much with the immigrants who preceded them and those who followed them to the new West.

Endnotes

1 Edward McIntosh was born on St. Valentine's day, 1784, in the Scottish highland town of Inverness.

2 All dollars in parenthesis are at 2019 values.

3 General Vallejo released the contents of Governor Figueroa's secret memo in the Californian newspaper on April 3, 1847, twelve years after its receipt.

4 Rancho Cañada de Jonive translates to Ranch of the Glen or Ravine Jonive. According to the *California Place Names of Indian Origin* (June 15, 1916): "Jonive, a grant in Sonoma County, has a name of unknown origin. The sound v is not Indian, in this vicinity; but might be Spanish orthography for b."

5 Rancho Cañada de Pogolimi: Ranch of the Glen or Ravine Pogolimi. Pogolimi or Pogolome is most likely a proper name or noun.

6 Rancho San Quentin: Ranch of Saint Quentin, originally Saint Quintin or Quentin of Amiens, an early Christian martyr.

7 Father Lootens is memorialized in Lootens Place in San Rafael, California.

8 Rancho Cañada de Herrera: Ranch of the Glen or Ravine Herrera. Most often written in the male form (*herrero*), *herrera* translates from Spanish as blacksmith.

Bibliography

Bancroft, H. H., *California Pioneer Register and Index, 1542–1848: Including Inhabitants of California, 1769-1800, and List of Pioneers: Extracted from History of California* (Baltimore, MD: Regional Publishing, 1964)

Burdell, C., "Novato Pioneers," *The Novato Historian*, vol 27. Number 2 (Nicasio, CA: Nicasio Historical Society, June 2003), pp. 1–4.

Dana, R. H., Jr., *Two Years Before the Mast: A Personal Narrative* (Boston, MA: Houghton Mifflin Company, 1911)

Devine, T. M., *To the Ends of the Earth: Scotland's Global Diaspora, 1750–2010* (London, England: Penguin Books, 2012)

Gibson, J. R., *Otter Skins, Boston Ships, and China Goods: The Maritime Fur Trade of the Northwest Coast, 1785–1841* (Seattle, WA: University of Washington Press, 1999)

Gibson, J. R., *California Through Russian Eyes, 1806–1848* (Norman, OK: The Arthur H. Clark Company/University of California Press, 2013)

Livingston, D., and Doss, E., *Nicasio: The Historic Valley at the Center of Marin* (Nicasio, CA: Nicasio Historical Society, 2008)

Marin Independent Journal, "Highlights of Marin's History, from 1850–2010" (San Rafael, CA: *Marin Independent Journal*), March 23, 2011

Mason, J. and Park, H. V., *Early Marin* (2nd ed.) (Inverness, CA: North Shore Books, 1976)

Mawn, G. F., *Jasper O'Farrell: Surveyor, Farmer, and Politico* (San Francisco, CA: Unpublished Thesis for the Degree of Master of Arts in History, University of San Francisco, 1970)

Munro-Fraser, J. P., *History of Marin County, California: Including Its Geography, Geology, Topography and Climatography, 1880* (London, England: Forgotten Books, 2018)

Ogden, A., *The California Sea Otter Trade, 1784–1848* (Berkeley, CA: University of California Press, 1941)

Pryor, A., *The Mexican Land Grants of California* (Roseville, CA: Stagecoach Publishing, 2011)

Royce, J. and Cleland, R. G., *California, from the Conquest in 1846 to the Second Vigilance Committee in San Francisco: A Study of American Character* (New York, NY: Alfred A. Knopf, 1948)

San Francisco Committee of Vigilance of 1856, *Constitution and Address of the Committee of Vigilance of San Francisco* (San Francisco, CA: Morning Globe Print, 1856)

Sinclair, M., *San Francisco: A Cultural and Literary History* (Oxford, England: Signal, 2004)

Stewart, G. R., *Committee of Vigilance: Revolution in San Francisco, 1851: An Account of The Hundred Days When Certain Citizens Undertook the Suppression of the Criminal Activities of the Sydney Ducks* (Boston, MA: Houghton Mifflin, 1964)

Spitz, B., *Marin: A History* (San Anselmo, CA: Potrero Meadow Publishing, 2006)

Thompson, R. A., *The Russian Settlement in California: Fort Ross: Founded 1812, Abandoned 1841; Why the Russians Came and Why They Left* (Oakland, CA: Biobook, 1951)

Williams, M. F., *Papers of the San Francisco Committee of Vigilance of 1851: Minutes and Miscellaneous Papers, Financial Accounts and Vouchers* (Berkeley, CA: University of California Press, 1919)

Woolfenden, J. and Elkinton, A., *Cooper: Juan Bautista Rogers Cooper, Sea Captain, Adventurer, Ranchero, and Early California Pioneer, 1791–1872* (Pacific Grove, CA: Boxwood Press, 1983)

About the Author

Jo M. Haraf's fiction and poetry have been published in the *California Writers Club Literary Review*, *Flash Fiction Magazine*, and *Ragnarok*. She edited and co-authored *Journal Across the Plains, 1852* (Fonthill, 2020), a history of the Verdenal family's 1852 wagon train journey from Missouri to California.

Jo earned her M.F.A. in creative writing at Pacific University. A regular speaker on the craft of writing, she is a proud member of the Historical Novel Society and the Biographers International Organization.

After residing in Marin, California, for a quarter of a century, she now lives on Florida's Suncoast with her husband and a scruffy terrier whose adoration sustains her through revisions and rejections.
www.JoHaraf.com